The Magic of Jelly

The Magic of Jelly

100 New & Favorite Recipes by Welch's

Sterling Publishing Co., Inc. New York
A Sterling/Chapelle Book

Chapelle, Ltd., Inc., P.O. Box 9252, Ogden, UT 84409
(801) 621-2777 Phone (801) 621-2788 Fax
e-mail: chapelle@chapelleltd.com
Web site: www.chapelleltd.com

Library of Congress Cataloging-in-Publication Data
The magic of jelly : 100 new & favorite recipes / by Welch's.
      p. cm.
   Includes index.
   ISBN 1-4027-2564-7
1.   Cookery (Jelly)   I. Welch's.

TX814.5.J35M35 2005
641.8'642--dc22

                                        2005013021

10 9 8 7 6 5 4 3
Published by Sterling Publishing Co., Inc.
387 Park Avenue South, New York, NY 10016
©2005 by Welch's®
Distributed in Canada by Sterling Publishing
c/o Canadian Manda Group, 165 Dufferin Street
Toronto, Ontario, Canada M6K 3H6
Distributed in Australia by Capricorn Link (Australia) Pty. Ltd.
P.O. Box 704, Windsor, NSW 2756, Australia
Printed and Bound in China

Sterling ISBN 1-4027-2564-7

For information about custom editions, special sales, premium and corporate purchases, please contact Sterling Special Sales Department at 800-805-5489 or specialsales@sterlingpub.com

Credits:

Editor:	Lecia Monsen
Book Design:	Matt Shay
Photography:	Ryne Hazen, Zac Williams
Photo Stylist:	Kim Monkres
Food Stylist:	Maxine Bramwell
Copy Editor:	Marilyn Goff

Table of Contents

Introduction

Introduction

In this cookbook, you'll find dozens of delicious recipes that will both nourish your family and entertain your guests. From Jellyroll Pancakes in the morning to Best Ever Monte Cristo sandwiches at lunch, to glazed ham and baked beans in the evening, you'll find recipes for any occasion.

Many people have grown up with Welch's and remember well the signature purple mustache of their youth, brought about after drinking a cool, tasty glass of grape juice. But chances are most don't really know much about how Welch's got its start. Let's take a step back in time and see if we can shed some light on how Welch's came to be one of the most trusted consumer brand names in American history.

How Welch's Got Its Start

In 1869, Dr. Welch and his son Charles, borrowing from the experiments of Dr. Louis Pasteur and working in the family's Vineland, New Jersey, kitchen, produced an "unfermented wine" or grape juice. The intent was to produce a nonalcoholic beverage that could be served at their church's communion service. Dr. Welch, though successful in his experiment, was unsuccessful in finding a viable outlet as church members expressed their preference for staying with wine.

When sales didn't materialize, story has it that Dr. Welch contemplated abandoning the venture. Letters to Charles indicate he wanted his son to pursue a career in dentistry instead of making grape juice. Fortunately for Welch's—and for us—Charles thought otherwise. Early on, Charles saw the power of marketing and applied it successfully to popularize the Welch's brand name and boost sales.

Thousands of thirsty Americans sampled "Dr. Welch's Grape Juice" at the Chicago World's Fair in 1893 and the beverage that had its humble beginnings in a New Jersey kitchen was well on its way to becoming a national favorite.

Over the years, Welch's Grape Juice (the "Dr." was dropped in 1893) has been served at state dinners in Washington, D.C., adopted as the beverage of choice by the Secretary of the Navy, and promoted as the sponsor of the popular children's television program, "The Howdy Doody Show."

Today, Welch's is one of the leading agricultural cooperatives in the United States and the number one manufacturer and marketer of Concord and Niagara grape-based products in the world. The company also produces a range of other fruit-based products—more than 400 in all—including, of course, its world-famous grape jelly.

A Few Words about the Concord and Niagara Grapes

Ephraim Wales Bull has been called the "father of the Concord grape," and rightfully so. Shortly after moving from Boston to Concord, Massachusetts, around the mid 1800s, Bull began experimenting with the native grapes he found in the area. A number of years and more than 20,000 cross-breeding experiments later, he found a vine that had the traces of the quality he sought.

In 1853, Bull exhibited the grape at the Massachusetts Horticultural Society's annual show. The following year he placed it on the market under the name of "Concord" after his adopted home town. Success was immediate and in a few years, the Concord had spread from Massachusetts to the Mississippi. Today, although most Concord grapes are grown in other areas of the United States, the descendant of the original Concord grape vine resides on the property once owned by Bull. And it's still producing grapes.

The Niagara, known by many as the Concord's golden-green cousin, is a cross between the Concord and the white Cassady grape. Viticulturists C. L. Hoag and B. W. Clark crossbred the two in 1868 and just four years later, their efforts bore fruit. The result: plump, luminescent grapes that changed from light green to delicate yellow as the growing season advanced. Today, the Niagara's sweet-to-tart flavor has earned it a reputation as one of America's leading grapes.

The Grape's Beginnings

As indebted as we are to the noble work of Messrs. Bull, Hoag, and Clark, we would be remiss not to acknowledge that the grape has actually been around for thousands of years. Grapes grew wild way back when, but didn't remain so for very long.

They were actually among the earliest cultivated fruits, with historical records indicating the vitis vinifera grape may have originated near the Black Sea and spread southward to the Middle East. Archaeologists believe these grapes were cultivated in Mesopotamia as early as 6000 B.C. From there, the grape spread eastward to Phoenicia and Egypt. By 2000 B.C., Phoenician sailors were transporting vines across the Mediterranean Sea to Greece and beyond.

People harvested grapes for winemaking from the beginning, but the ancient Greeks were the first to make a serious practice of grape growing and winemaking. However, with no refrigeration, uncontrolled fermentation, and the lack of sanitation, their dark syrupy wines were, at best, an acquired taste.

The Romans soon refined the art of grape growing and processing. They introduced pruning by knife and proper filtering and storage. The Romans studied the effects of climate, soil, and pruning on grape flavor. The art declined along with Roman civilization, but monks kept the practice alive in the medieval abbeys of France and Germany.

As knowledge of plant biology, grafting, and hybridization broadened, so did the varieties of grapes and their uses. Soon "table" and "dessert" grapes were harvested, followed by grapes for raisins.

Not until the pioneering work of Dr. Thomas Bramwell Welch in 1869 would unfermented processed grape juice become a popular beverage that even, on occasion, supplanted wine.

Finally, in the twentieth century, Welch's brought its jams and jellies into the picture, many of which star in the recipes you'll see in this cookbook.

Welch's Timeline

1806
Ephraim Bull, "the father of the Concord grape," is born in Boston on March 4.

1825
Thomas Bramwell Welch, who pioneered the fruit juice processing business in the United States and founded the company that bears his name, is born in Glastonbury, England, on December 31.

1853
The Concord grape—the product of 22,000 crossbreeding experiments—makes its debut at the Massachusetts Horticultural Society.

1868
C. L. Hoag and B. W. Clark crossbreed the Concord with the Cassady grape to produce the first American green grape. Four years later, the grape is perfected and marketed as the Niagara grape.

1869
Dr. Welch and son Charles gather Concord grapes outside their Vineland, New Jersey, home and, borrowing from the pasteurization work of Dr. Louis Pasteur, succeed in producing an "unfermented grape wine" (aka, grape juice).

1882
Charles E. Welch creates C. E. Welch and Co., to market and sell "Dr. Welch's Unfermented Wine."

1893
Thousands give Welch's the "thumbs up" after tasting samples of the company's grape juice at the Chicago World's Fair. Charles would later write: "Here seemed to be the beginning of things coming our way."

1913
William Jennings Bryan, the teetotaling Secretary of State under President Wilson, serves Welch's grape juice instead of wine at a dinner honoring the British ambassador.

1914
Secretary of the Navy Josephus Daniels causes an uproar when he bans alcoholic beverages from the Navy and offers as a substitute Welch's grape juice.

1923
Welch's develops and markets its now famous Concord Grape Jelly.

1926

Charles E. Welch, who had been the guiding spirit behind Welch's and one of the primary movers in the Concord grape industry, dies on January 6.

1927

The company's first non-grape product, Welch's Homogenized Tomato Juice, is introduced.

1934

Welch's begins its eleven-year sponsorship of the "Irene Rich Show," one of the most popular programs in the early days of radio.

1945

Jack Kaplan purchases the controlling interest of The Welch Grape Juice Company and becomes its president.

1949

A pioneer in the frozen juice concentrate business, Welch's introduces its Frozen Grape Juice Concentrate to consumers.

1953

Welch's introduces the first in its long-running series of jelly tumblers, featuring Howdy Doody.

1955

Welch's begins sponsorship of "Walt Disney's Mickey Mouse Club" and establishes a grape juice concession stand at Disneyland.

1956

The National Grape Cooperative Association acquires Welch's and establishes a two-board system to oversee both agricultural and manufacturing-marketing activities.

1972

Two new 100% grape juice products are introduced: Welch's Red Grape Juice and Welch's White Grape Juice.

1985

Welch's introduces jellies and preserves in squeezable containers—a first for the jellies and jams category.

1994

Recalling its heritage and family tradition, Welch's launches a new advertising campaign called "Memories" and featuring child actor Travis Tedford.

1996

A U.S. Department of Agriculture study finds that Welch's Purple 100% Grape Juice has three times the natural antioxidant power of other natural juices, including orange, apple, and grapefruit.

1998

Everyone knows Winnie the Pooh, but not even the folks at Welch's knew how successful Winnie would be as the lovable bear becomes the top-selling character in Welch's jelly glass collection.

2002

With distribution in more than 40 countries and territories around the globe, Welch's expands into two more countries—the United Kingdom and South Korea.

2003

Welch's celebrates the 150th anniversary of the Concord grape and its growers harvest a near-record crop of more than 300,000 tons.

2004

The Travel Channel features Welch's in a segment on one of its new shows, "John Ratzenberger's Made in America."

Welch's Today

Welch's is the processing and marketing arm of the National Grape Cooperative Association, Inc., whose more than 1,300 patrons supply its principal raw products—Concord and Niagara grapes—from nearly 50,000 acres of vineyards in Pennsylvania, Michigan, New York, Ohio, Washington, and Ontario, Canada.

The purpose of the company is to build the long-term value of the cooperative, to release that value back to the growers over time, and to provide a reliable market for their grapes through excellence in product quality, customer service, market responsiveness, and consumer satisfaction.

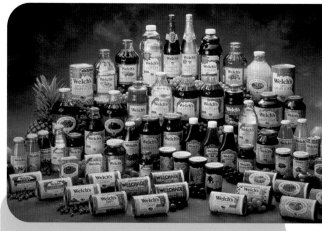

Welch's had its beginnings in 1869 when Dr. Thomas Bramwell Welch successfully processed an unfermented Concord grape wine that could be used in his church's communion service. Applying the theory of Louis Pasteur to pasteurize his juice, Welch unknowingly opened the gateway for all fruit juice processing in the United States.

Now headquartered in Concord, Massachusetts, Welch's is the world's leading marketer of Concord and Niagara grape-based products, including grape juice and jelly. The company also produces a variety of other fruit-based products, including 100% juices and juice cocktails in the following forms: bottled, refrigerated, single-serve, and frozen and shelf-stable concentrates. In addition, Welch's produces an assortment of jams, jellies, and preserves.

These products are sold by the food store, special markets, industrial, and military, licensing and international divisions throughout the United States and in some 40 countries around the world.

While the juice, jam, and jelly made from Welch's Concord grapes are deliciously familiar to most of us, you may not know that grape juice made from Concord grapes and white grape juice made with Niagara grapes has been studied by researchers for more than a decade.

- Welch's 100% Grape Juices and 100% White Grape Juices have no added sugar. The Concord and Niagara grapes that make up these Welch's Juices are naturally sweet!

- Drinking Welch's 100% Grape Juice helps promote a healthy heart and arteries. That's because it's made from Welch's deep, dark, antioxidant-rich Concord Grapes.

- Welch's 100% Grape Juice from Concord Grapes has no fat and no cholesterol and is certified by the American Heart Association (AHA) as a heart-healthy juice, as evidenced by the AHA's heart check mark that appears on the packaging.

- Welch's 100% Grape Juice has natural antioxidant power—in fact, more than twice the natural antioxidant power of orange juice!

Grapevine to Store Shelf

Let's take a quick trip with a box full of grapes from the sunny vineyard through a Welch's plant and into the supermarket.

The journey really begins in the vineyards of the more than 1,300 grape growers who supply Welch's with Concord and Niagara grapes. Aided by expert horticulturalists, growers are constantly striving to improve the quality of their grapes. Welch's standards are high, and growers know that grapes given the best of care make products that will satisfy an increasingly demanding consumer public.

At the peak of ripeness, usually at the end of September and through October, the grapes are harvested. Almost 99% of the harvesting today is done by mechanical harvesters, large machines that pass over the vine and literally vibrate the grapes from their stems into troughs.

The mechanical harvesters automatically empty the grapes from the troughs into one-ton boxes, which are carried by truck immediately to a Welch's plant. Here a federal inspector carefully scrutinizes the grapes to ensure they meet rigid sugar solids and color standards. This is the first of many such inspections.

The grapes are then weighed and delivered to a receiving area where a rotating forklift truck removes the one-ton boxes from the truck and empties them into a hopper.

From the hopper, the grapes are transported to a large destemming machine. Here, huge revolving perforated cylinders agitate the grapes and paddles push them through holes into a collecting trough. These holes are just big enough for the grapes; the few stems that the mechanical harvester may have collected won't go through. The grapes and juice,

collected in a trough below the destemming machine, are pumped to a receiving tank.

From this tank the grapes are fed into a heated vat. The heat brings out the full rich color and flavor of the Concord grapes. From here, the mixture is pumped into hot collecting tanks where the grapes are agitated and transferred to a dejuicer. At this point, the grapes are in a slurry-type mixture and the dejuicer screens out the free juice from the pulp, skins, and seeds.

This "free run" juice is fed into another collecting tank. The juice is then filtered and pumped through continuous heat exchangers where it is heated briefly to a temperature of 185°F. It remains at this temperature just a short time—longer exposure would spoil the delicate aroma and color. Then it goes through another machine that chills it almost to the freezing point. The juice is now completely pasteurized; the microorganisms that could cause fermentation have been destroyed. It is then stored in large refrigerated tanks.

Meanwhile, the dejuiced grapes are sent through a series of presses where all remaining juice is removed. This juice is also filtered, put through the same pasteurization process, and pumped into storage tanks.

Welch's **Grapelade**
PURE GRAPE JAM

Welch's Pure Fruit Delicacies
From the Fruit Lands of Niagara.

Whether it involves spreads, juices, frozen or shelf-stable concentrates, sparkling cocktails, or any of the hundreds of other items in the Welch's line, a great diversity of skills and abilities are employed in processing and selling the products the company manufactures. In all operations of its business, Welch's is dedicated to producing and distributing the finest quality products and providing the best possible service to customers.

for PURE enjoyment

There's only one Welch's . . . for better fruit juices, jams, jellies and preserves . . . famous since 1869

Making Welch's Jelly

To make jelly, grape juice is drawn from large storage tanks and piped into a cookroom where it enters a stainless-steel batching kettle. Here, other ingredients, mainly sugar and corn syrup, are added according to a predetermined formula and the mixture is blended. This mixture is then piped into a vacuum kettle, where pectin is added. After a short cook period under high vacuum, only the grape jelly remains.

All during this processing operation, frequent quality checks are made. The jelly enters finishing kettles where it is inspected again as the last step before going to automatic filling lines to be put into jars and squeezable bottles. Similar processes are used to make jams and fruit spreads.

Fun Facts for Kids

What are grapes?

Grapes are berries that grow in clusters on woody vines. Each vine branches out and climbs whatever wall, fence, or other vertical surface it grows near with its curling tendrils. The fruit grows from buds that sprout on the vine.

Where did the first grapes grow?

No one knows for sure where the wild grape first took root, but archeologists speculate that grapes originated near the Black Sea, which is at the southeastern tip of Europe, southwest of Russia. Grapes were first cultivated in the Middle East. In ancient history, grapes were considered the food of the gods and were found in Egyptian tombs.

Where do Welch's grapes come from?

Welch's grape jams, jellies, juices, and other treats come from two kinds of grapes: the Concord and the Niagara. The purple Concord grape was developed in Concord, Massachusetts, in 1853 at a farm not far from the homes of famed writers Nathaniel Hawthorne and Louisa May Alcott. The green Niagara grape came later, invented in Niagara County, New York, in 1868. Today our grapes are grown in Michigan, New York, Ohio, Pennsylvania, Washington, and Ontario, Canada.

How are grapes grown?

Grape vines are planted near a trellis, or latticed fence, for support. In the spring, buds on the grapevine swell, open, and begin to grow. During this time, growers must protect the plants from frost, insects, and mold. They must also prune, or trim, the vines to give each plant the space it needs to ripen into a full-flavored, rich-colored berry. Ground cover is laid around the vines to reduce dust and prevent weeds.

What is the difference between grape jelly and grape jam?

Both grape jelly and jam are made from grapes that have been sweetened and mixed with pectin, which causes the jelly or jam to become a thick gel. Grape jelly is made from grape juice, while jam is made from crushed grapes. Usually you can see the seeds in jam, but Grape Jelly is clear of seeds.

In fact, the first mention of the sandwich came during World War II, when peanut butter and jelly sandwiches became part of the U.S. military rations. At that time, foods that were rich in protein, such as meat and milk, as well as other commodities were very expensive and the supply was limited. People turned to the protein and vitamin-rich peanut butter and jelly sandwich for fulfilling, nutritious, low-cost meals—then found they loved the taste.

The sandwich quickly became an incredibly popular source of nutrition among American families—a trend that never went away.

How big was the world's largest peanut butter and jelly sandwich?

Forty feet long. That's about 10 seven-year-old children lined up head-to-toe. The sandwich was made with 150 pounds of peanut butter and 50 pounds of jelly. It was created on November 6, 1993, in Peanut, Pennsylvania.

What came first, peanut butter or jelly?

Jelly. Although peanut butter was invented in 1895, it didn't hit store shelves until 1914. Meanwhile, jelly had a running start. Jams and jellies had been made for centuries—first in Middle Eastern countries, then in Europe.

Where did the peanut butter and jelly sandwich come from?

The purple Concord grape jelly many people today associate with the traditional peanut butter and jelly sandwich was introduced by Welch's in 1923, just two years before Joseph Rosefield founded Skippy. But historians would not mention the peanut butter and jelly sandwich until the 1940s.

Morning Starters
Chapter 1

Strawberry Breakfast Smoothie

1 container (8 oz.) plain yogurt

¼ cup Welch's® Strawberry Spread

1 banana, sliced

4 ice cubes

1. In blender, mix yogurt, Welch's®
   Strawberry Spread, and banana.

2. Add ice cubes and blend
   until smooth.

3. Pour into tall glass.

Variation:

Garnish with strawberry or mint sprig.

Tip:

Add a scoop of protein
powder to thicken.

French-toasted Ham Sandwiches

12 thin slices white bread

6 slices ham

3 eggs, well beaten

½ cup milk

¼ tsp. salt

Dash of ground black pepper

Butter

Welch's® Grape Jelly

1. For each sandwich, place one ham slice between two slices of bread. Set aside.

2. Combine eggs, milk, salt, and pepper in a shallow dish. Mix well.

3. Dip each sandwich into mixture, thoroughly coating each side.

4. In a skillet, heat butter; slowly sauté sandwiches on both sides, making certain that filling is thoroughly heated and sandwiches are brown. Serve with Welch's® Grape Jelly.

Grape Puff-wiches

4 servings

3 egg whites

¼ cup granulated sugar

⅛ tsp. cinnamon

⅛ tsp. allspice

8 slices raisin bread

¼ cup butter

½ cup Welch's® Grape Jelly

1. Beat egg whites until they form soft peaks.

2. Slowly add sugar and spices, continuing to beat. Set aside.

3. Toast raisin bread until golden brown.

4. Spread one slice with butter and Welch's® Grape Jelly. Top with additional slice of toast. Spread top of sandwich with butter and Welch's® Grape Jelly. Repeat with remaining bread slices.

5. Top with beaten egg white mixture. Broil sandwiches until golden brown. Serve warm.

Western-wich

English muffin

Butter

2 eggs

4 slices bacon, cooked

Welch's® Grape Jam

1. Split English muffin in half; toast until golden brown. Butter.

2. Scramble two eggs.

3. Top each muffin half with scrambled eggs, strips of crisp bacon, and a generous spoonful of Welch's® Grape Jam.

Waffle Grape-wich

2 frozen waffles

Peanut butter

Welch's® Grape Jam

1. Toast waffles until golden brown.

2. While still warm, spread with peanut butter.

3. In a saucepan, heat Welch's Grape® Jam and spoon over waffles.

Jellyroll Pancakes

12 pancakes

1 cup milk

2 Tbsp. butter, melted

2 eggs, beaten

1 cup all-purpose flour, sifted

1 tsp. baking powder

¼ tsp. salt

Welch's® Grape Jelly

Confectioners sugar

1. In a saucepan, heat milk and butter. Cool slightly.

2. Beat in eggs, flour, baking powder, and salt; continue beating until smooth.

3. Pour ¼ cup of the batter onto lightly greased, heated skillet. Cook until brown. Turn and brown remaining side.

4. While warm, spread with Welch's® Grape Jelly; roll up. Dust with confectioners sugar.

Eggs in Toast Cups

6 servings

6 eggs

⅓ cup light cream

1 tsp. salt

¼ tsp. ground black pepper

12 slices white bread, crusts removed

Butter

¾ cup Welch's® Grape Jelly

1. Preheat oven to 400°F.

2. Butter both sides of sliced bread and press each into a muffin-tin cup.

3. Bake 10 to 15 minutes.

4. In a bowl, beat eggs. Add cream, salt, and pepper; beat until blended.

5. In a skillet, heat butter. Add egg mixture and stir over low heat until eggs are firm but creamy.

6. Remove all cups to platter and place 1 tablespoon Welch's® Grape Jelly into each cup. Fill with scrambled eggs. Serve immediately.

Creamy Crescents

1 package (8 oz.) refrigerated crescent dinner rolls

1 round Brie cheese, room temperature

Welch's® Grape Jam

Brown sugar

¼ cup maple syrup

1. Preheat oven to 350°F.

2. Roll out crescent rolls and spread with Brie.

3. Spread Welch's® Grape Jam on Brie; roll crescents back up.

4. Drizzle maple syrup over rolls. Sprinkle brown sugar on top.

5. Bake 25 minutes. Let cool for 10 minutes before serving.

Noodle Charlotte

6 squares

¼ cup butter

1 package (8 oz.) medium noodles, cooked and drained

4 eggs, well beaten

½ cup light cream

1 Tbsp. granulated sugar

½ cup Welch's® Grape Jelly

1. Preheat oven to 400°F.

2. Melt butter in an 8-inch square pan; add noodles.

3. Beat eggs, cream, and sugar until fluffy. Pour over noodles.

4. Bake 35 to 40 minutes, or until top is browned.

5. Cut into 6 squares and top each with a spoonful of Welch's® Grape Jelly.

Tip:

Serve with chicken, lamb, or ham.

Surprise Muffins

12 muffins

3 cups all-purpose flour

4 tsp. double-acting baking powder

½ cup granulated sugar

1 tsp. salt

¼ cup butter

3 eggs, well beaten

1½ cups milk

1 cup golden seedless raisins

½ cup Welch's® Grape Jelly

1. Preheat oven to 375°F.

2. In a large bowl, sift together flour, baking powder, sugar, and salt. Cut in butter.

3. Mix eggs, milk, and raisins; blend into flour mixture. Stir lightly just to dampen flour. (If too dry, add a few drops more milk.)

4. Fill greased muffin pans one-third full of batter.

5. Place 1 teaspoon Welch's® Grape Jelly on top of batter in each muffin cup, and cover with remaining batter so that cups are not more than two-thirds full.

6. Bake 20 minutes, or until tested done. Serve warm.

Jam-packed Muffins

12 muffins

2 cups all-purpose flour

⅓ cup granulated sugar

1 Tbsp. baking powder

½ tsp. salt

½ cup peanut butter

1 cup milk

1 egg

¼ cup vegetable oil

½ cup Welch's® Grape Jam

1. Preheat oven to 400°F.

2. In a large bowl, sift together flour, sugar, baking powder, and salt.

3. Add peanut butter; mix until crumbly. Add milk, egg, and oil; mix until blended.

4. Spoon half of the batter into 12 paper-lined muffin cups, dividing equally.

5. Spoon 1 tablespoon Welch's® Grape Jam into center of each muffin. Cover with remaining batter.

6. Bake 18 to 20 minutes, until lightly browned. Serve warm or at room temperature.

Strawberry-Citrus Muffins

16 muffins

2¼ cups all-purpose flour

2 tsp. baking powder

1 tsp. baking soda

½ tsp. salt

¾ cup granulated sugar

½ cup milk

½ cup sour cream

⅓ cup vegetable oil

1 egg

1 Tbsp. orange zest, finely grated

1 cup fresh strawberries, thinly sliced to ⅛-inch

⅓ cup Welch's® Strawberry Spread

1. Preheat oven to 375°F.

2. Butter standard muffin tins.

3. In a large bowl, sift together flour, baking powder, baking soda, and salt. Set aside.

4. In a medium bowl, whisk together sugar, milk, sour cream, oil, egg, and orange zest until mixed.

5. Add wet mixture to dry ingredients. Stir just until blended. Stir in strawberries.

6. Place a spoonful of batter into each prepared muffin cup. Top each with a scant teaspoon of Welch's® Strawberry Spread. Spoon the remaining batter over the Welch's® Strawberry Spread, filling each cup about two-thirds full.

7. Bake 15 to 18 minutes, or until done.

8. Cool in tins for 5 minutes before removing.

Tip:

Pat strawberries dry between paper towels before adding to batter to keep juices from coloring batter.

Special Corn Muffins

12 muffins

¾ cup cornmeal

1 cup all-purpose flour

4 tsp. baking powder

1 tsp. salt

4 Tbsp. granulated sugar

1 egg, well beaten

1 cup milk

3 Tbsp. vegetable oil

12 tsp Welch's® Grape Jam or Welch's® Grape Jelly

1. Preheat oven to 425°F.

2. In large bowl, sift cornmeal, flour, baking powder, salt, and sugar together.

3. Combine beaten egg, milk, and melted shortening. Stir into dry mixture.

4. Fill greased muffin pans two-thirds full of batter.

5. Place 1 teaspoon Welch's® Grape Jelly or Jam on top of batter in each muffin cup.

6. Bake 25 minutes, or until tested done.

Jammin' Cornmeal Muffins

12 muffins

½ cup cornmeal

1½ cups buttermilk

2¼ cups all-purpose flour

1 cup granulated sugar

½ tsp. baking powder

¾ tsp. baking soda

½ tsp. salt

3 eggs, lightly beaten

¾ cup butter, melted

Welch's® Strawberry Spread

1. Preheat oven to 375°F.

2. Combine cornmeal and buttermilk; let stand for 10 minutes.

3. In large bowl, sift together flour, sugar, baking powder, baking soda, and salt.

4. Add cornmeal mixture, eggs, and melted butter, stirring just until moistened.

5. Spoon batter into muffin tins lined with paper baking cups, filling each just to top of paper liner.

6. With small spoon, shape well in center of each muffin. Fill each well with 1 teaspoon Welch's® Strawberry Spread.

7. Bake 20 to 25 minutes.

Orange-Grape Muffins

14 muffins

2 cups all-purpose flour

1 Tbsp. double-acting baking powder

½ tsp. salt

¼ cup granulated sugar

½ tsp. ground nutmeg

1 egg

¾ cup milk

¼ cup orange juice

1 Tbsp. orange zest, finely grated

¼ cup vegetable or canola oil

Welch's® Grape Jam

1. Preheat oven to 375°F.

2. In a large bowl, sift together flour, baking powder, salt, sugar, and nutmeg into a bowl.

3. Beat egg until frothy. Stir in milk, orange juice, and zest. Stir in shortening.

4. Make well in flour mixture; add milk mixture all at once. Stir quickly, until mixed but still lumpy.

5. Fill greased 2½-inch muffin cups about two-thirds full.

6. Bake 25 minutes, or until tested done.

7. Remove from oven; top each muffin with a heaping teaspoon of Welch's® Grape Jam.

8. Keep muffins warm in foil or bread warmer.

Lunchbox

Chapter 2

Best Ever Monte Cristo Sandwiches

8 slices white bread

4 thin slices ham

4 thick slices chicken, breast

4 thick slices Swiss cheese

2 eggs

1 cup milk

2 Tbsp. all-purpose flour

1 tsp. salt

¼ tsp. ground black pepper

Butter

½ cup sour cream

½ cup Welch's® Grape Jelly

1. Make sandwiches, using 2 slices bread and 1 slice each of ham, chicken, and cheese.

2. Beat together eggs, milk, flour, salt, and pepper.

3. Dip sandwiches in egg mixture.

4. Fry in butter in heavy skillet until golden brown on all sides mixed together.

Serve immediately with sour cream and Welch's® Grape Jelly.

Spicy Grape-wich

1 serving

Crusty roll

Dill pickle relish

3 slices crisp bacon

Welch's® Grape Jelly

1. Split roll and spread with pickle relish.

2. Layer bacon slices.

3. Top bacon with Welch's® Grape Jelly.

Deviled Ham-wich

1 serving

1 can (2 oz.) deviled ham
Green onion, chopped (to taste)
1 slice whole wheat bread
Cheddar cheese, grated
Welch's® Concord Grape Jelly

1. Mix canned deviled ham with chopped onion; spread on bread.
2. Sprinkle with grated cheddar cheese.
3. Broil until warm and lightly browned.
4. Top with Welch's® Concord Grape Jelly.

Mix-wich

4–6 sandwiches

1 package (8 oz.) cream cheese

3 Tbsp. Welch's® Grape Jam

⅓ cup pecans, finely chopped

Bread of choice

1. Using an electric mixer, thoroughly blend together cream cheese, Welch's® Grape Jam, and pecans.

2. Spread on slices of white, rye, whole wheat, date-and-nut bread or bagels.

Tropical Grape-wich

1 serving

2 slices white bread

Whipped cream cheese

Pineapple tidbits

Pecans, chopped

Welch's® Grape Jelly

1. Spread a slice of white bread generously with whipped cream cheese.

2. Garnish with pineapple tidbits and pecans.

3. Top with Welch's® Grape Jelly and remaining bread slice.

Extra-Special PBJ

3 Tbsp. extra-crunchy peanut butter

2 Tbsp. Welch's® Grape Jam or Welch's® Grape Jelly

2 Tbsp. marshmallow cream

4 slices sandwich bread

1 Tbsp. unsalted butter, softened

1. In a small mixing bowl, combine the peanut butter, Welch's® Grape Jam or Welch's® Grape Jelly, and marshmallow cream.

2. Stir with a spoon just until the peanut butter is swirled around with the marshmallow cream and Welch's® Grape Jam.

3. Divide the peanut butter mixture between 2 slices of bread, spreading evenly.

4. Top with remaining bread slices.

5. Spread both sides of each sandwich with butter.

6. Heat a large skillet over medium high heat and add the sandwiches.

7. Cook until golden brown, about 2 minutes per side.

8. Remove from heat and serve.

Grape Chicken-wich

1 serving

1 roll

Butter

Sliced chicken

Welch's® Grape Jam

1. Split roll in half; butter.

2. Place chicken in roll.

3. Top chicken with Welch's® Grape Jam.

Energy Squares

24 squares

1½ cups all-purpose flour

½ tsp. baking soda

½ tsp. salt

1 cup unsalted butter, room temperature

1 cup brown sugar, firmly packed

1 cup creamy or chunky peanut butter

1½ cups old-fashioned rolled oats

1 cup Welch's® Grape Jam or
Welch's® Grape Jelly

¼ cup toasted wheat germ (optional)

1. Preheat oven to 375°F and grease 9 x 13-inch pan.

2. Mix flour, baking soda, and salt; set aside.

3. In a large bowl, beat butter and brown sugar, at
   high speed, until creamy.

4. Beat in peanut butter until blended.

5. Reduce speed to low; blend in flour mixture and oats.

6. Spread two-thirds of the batter into pan
   with spatula.

7. Spread Welch's® Grape Jam or Welch's® Grape
   Jelly carefully over batter; sprinkle with wheat germ,
   if desired.

8. Spoon out small dollops of remaining batter, and
   scatter over jam.

9. Bake 25 minutes, until golden. The squares will be
   bubbly and still look soft.

for PURE enjoyment

Crispy Rice-wiches

Approximately 15 squares

6 cups crispy rice cereal

¾ cup granulated sugar

¾ cup light corn syrup

¾ cup peanut butter

¾ cup Welch's® Grape Jelly

1. Line a cookie sheet with plastic wrap.

2. Pour cereal into large bowl. Combine sugar and corn syrup in medium saucepan. Stirring occasionally, bring to boil over medium heat.

3. Boil for 1 minute. Remove from heat.

4. Stir in peanut butter until smooth. Pour over cereal; stir to coat.

5. Press evenly into prepared cookie sheet. Wait 5 minutes; then cut the mixture in half widthwise.

6. Spread Welch's® Grape Jelly on half of the mixture, then place the other half on top to make a sandwich.

7. Cut into squares.

Peanutty Jam S'mores

4 servings

Creamy or chunky peanut butter

Welch's® Grape Jam

4 full graham crackers, divided in half

Mini marshmallows

1. Evenly spread peanut butter and Welch's® Grape Jam on graham crackers.

2. Top with marshmallows.

3. Broil until marshmallows are golden brown. Top with remaining cracker halves.

Dinner Temptations
Chapter 3

Zesty Grape Dressing

1½ cups dressing

¾ cup vegetable oil

¼ cup white or red wine vinegar

1 tsp. salt

Dash of ground black pepper

½ tsp dry mustard

½ cup Welch's® Grape Jelly, melted

1. In a glass jar, combine all ingredients; cover tightly and shake to blend.

2. Chill. Shake again before pouring.

Sunburst Waldorf Salad

4–6 servings

3 cups apples, peeled, cored, and diced

¼ cup lemon juice

1 cup celery, diced

⅓ cup walnuts, chopped

Iceberg lettuce, shredded

3 navel oranges, peeled and sectioned

⅓ cup Welch's® Grape Jelly

½ cup mayonnaise

2 Tbsp. Welch's® Grape Juice

1. In a large bowl, combine apples and lemon juice.

2. Add celery and walnuts to bowl and toss. Place on a bed of shredded lettuce.

3. Surround salad with orange sections.

4. Spoon tiny bits of Welch's® Grape Jelly over apple mixture and chill until ready to serve.

5. Mix mayonnaise and Welch's® Grape Juice. Serve with salad.

Strawberry-Balsamic Dressing

2½ cups dressing

1 cup Welch's® Strawberry Spread

¼ cup balsamic vinegar

¼ cup Dijon mustard

½ to 1 tsp. ground black pepper, or to taste

½ cup olive oil

½ cup water

1. In a medium bowl, whisk together Welch's® Strawberry Spread, vinegar, mustard, and pepper, until thoroughly emulsified.
2. Gradually whisk in olive oil, then water.

Tip:

Serve with your favorite fruit salad using melon, peaches, blueberries, apricots, pineapple, cherries, or any fresh fruit in season.

Dressy Fruit Salad Sauce

¾ cup sauce

½ cup mayonnaise

1 Tbsp. vinegar

¼ cup Welch's® Grape Jelly

1. Beat mayonnaise with Welch's® Grape Jelly and vinegar until well blended.

Tip:

Combine with prepared fruit and serve in lettuce cups.

Sweet & Sour Sauce

1 cup sauce

½ cup Welch's® Grape Jelly

2 Tbsp. soy sauce

1 Tbsp. Worcestershire sauce

½ cup red wine vinegar

1. In a saucepan, combine all ingredients and simmer five minutes, stirring constantly.

Tips

Serve with hot roast beef, lamb, or pork chops. Also try with cooked cauliflower, beets, or carrots.

Sweet Tomato Pasta Sauce

6–8 servings

2 lbs. ground beef

1 Tbsp. vegetable oil

1 can (14 oz.) stewed tomatoes

1 jar (16 oz.) of spaghetti sauce

1 envelope onion soup mix

1 can (6 oz.) vegetable juice

½ cup Welch's® Grape Jelly

1. Brown meat in oil. Crumble with fork. Drain fat.

2. Add tomatoes, spaghetti sauce, onion soup mix, juice, and Welch's® Grape Jelly. Do not let the mixture boil.

3. Cook over medium heat for 30 minutes, stirring gently.

Tip:

Serve over pasta.

Concord Sauce

2 cups

½ cup Welch's® Concord Grape Jelly

1 tsp. orange zest, grated

2 tsp. sherry

1 cup heavy cream

2 tsp. confectioners sugar

1 tsp. vanilla extract

1. In a saucepan, combine Welch's® Concord Grape Jelly, orange zest, and sherry.

2. Simmer over low heat, stirring constantly. Cool.

3. Whip cream until fluffy; beat in confectioners sugar and vanilla.

4. Pour grape mixture over cream and ripple slightly by running a fork through mixture.

5. Chill until ready to use.

Tip:

Spoon over vanilla ice cream on orange chiffon cake, banana ice cream on angel food cake, fresh fruit compote, salad, or baked apples.

Jam Dippin' Good Sauce

1⅓ cups sauce

½ cup Welch's® Grape Juice

½ cup Welch's® Grape Jelly

⅓ cup chutney, chopped

1 Tbsp. red wine vinegar

1. Combine all ingredients in a saucepan and simmer until slightly thickened.

Tip:

Spoon over spareribs, shrimp, fried won tons, or egg rolls.

Sweet & Smoky Sauce

2½ cups sauce

4 strips bacon, diced

1 cup Welch's® Grape Jelly

½ cup onion, chopped

1 cup ketchup

2 Tbsp. cider vinegar

1. Sauté bacon and onions in saucepan until bacon is crisp. Drain fat.

2. Add remaining ingredients and cook over low heat for 10 minutes or until sauce thickens, stirring occasionally.

Tip:

Serve with grilled steak or meatballs.

Baked Beans

6–8 servings

48 oz. white or navy beans, cooked

4 strips bacon

1 large onion, finely chopped

⅓ cup Welch's® Grape Jam

½ cup ketchup

½ tsp. dry mustard

1. Preheat oven to 325°F.

2. Fry bacon until crisp. Remove bacon to paper towels, reserving fat in skillet. Crumble bacon strips.

3. Sauté onion in bacon fat; add Welch's® Grape Jam, ketchup, and mustard.

4. In a two-quart bean pot, combine beans, bacon, and onion mixture. Stir well.

5. Cover and bake 45 to 60 minutes.

Glazed Carrots

10 to 12 carrots

1 Tbsp. butter

½ cup Welch's® Grape Jam

2 Tbsp. lemon juice

½ tsp. lemon zest, grated

¼ tsp. ginger, minced

2 Tbsp. pecans, toasted and chopped

1. Peel carrots and cut on the diagonal into 2-inch pieces.

2. Cook until crisp tender in lightly salted water. Drain.

3. Combine butter, Welch's® Grape Jam, lemon juice, lemon zest, and ginger in a saucepan.

4. Add carrots.

5. Cook for 10 minutes over moderate heat, turning often to thoroughly glaze carrots.

6. Garnish with pecans.

Baked Ham with Strawberry Glaze

8–10 servings

1 fully cooked smoked ham (about 5 lbs.)

1½ cups Welch's® Strawberry Spread

⅓ cup prepared mustard

¼ cup lemon juice

1. Preheat oven to 325°F.

2. With a sharp knife, score fat surface, making uniform diagonal cuts about ⅛-inch deep and ¾-inch apart.

3. Place ham, fat side up, on rack in a shallow roasting pan.

4. Bake 1¼ to 2¼ hours.

5. In a small saucepan, combine Welch's® Strawberry Spread, mustard, and lemon juice; cook over low heat, stirring until blended.

6. During last 20 minutes of baking time, brush ham with about ½ cup glaze.

7. Let ham stand 10 minutes for easier slicing.

8. Heat remaining glaze and serve as a sauce for the ham.

Turkey Meatballs with Sweet & Spicy Sauce

4–6 servings

Sauce

2 Tbsp. hoisin sauce

2 Tbsp. ketchup

1 tsp. rice vinegar

¼ cup Welch's® Grape Jelly

1 tsp. soy sauce

Meatballs

1 lb. ground turkey

2 tsp. fresh ginger, minced

2 cloves garlic, minced

¼ tsp. red pepper, crushed

½ tsp. salt

1 egg white

½ cup cornstarch

½ cup all-purpose flour

2 cups vegetable oil

Sauce

1. In a small saucepan over medium heat, combine all sauce ingredients.

2. Heat to a boil; reduce to low. Stir until sauce thickens.

3. Remove from heat and cover to keep warm during meatball preparation.

Meatballs

1. In medium bowl, combine ground turkey with ginger, garlic, red pepper, salt, and egg white. Mix well.

2. Form into 1½-inch balls and set on waxed paper.

3. After all balls are formed, mix cornstarch and flour in a small bowl.

4. Roll each ball in the mixture. Return to waxed paper.

5. Heat oil in a deep frying pan or wok to 365°F.

6. Fry meatballs in batches for about 4 minutes, or until browned and cooked through.

7. Drain meatballs on paper towels. Transfer meatballs to a platter and serve with sauce.

Variation:

Meatballs can be baked, if desired.

Saucy & Sweet Chicken

4–6 servings

1 cup Welch's® Grape Juice

1 cup Welch's® Grape Jam

2 Tbsp. cornstarch

1 Tbsp. dry mustard

¼ cup water

3 lbs. broiler-fryer chicken, quartered

All-purpose flour

Salt to taste

Ground black pepper to taste

⅓ cup vegetable oil

2 sprigs fresh rosemary

2 Tbsp. balsamic vinegar

1. In a saucepan, combine Welch's® Grape Juice and Welch's® Grape Jam. Cook over low heat, stirring constantly, until smooth.

2. Blend cornstarch and mustard with water and set aside.

3. Dip chicken in flour seasoned with salt and pepper.

4. Brown chicken in hot oil, turning occasionally.

5. Drain excess oil from the pan.

6. Add grape sauce; cover and simmer slowly until chicken is done (about 45 minutes). Baste frequently with sauce.

7. Remove chicken to a plate and keep warm.

8. Stir cornstarch mixture, rosemary and vinegar into grape sauce and cook until slightly thckened. Pour over chicken.

Strawberry-Balsamic Chicken

4 servings

1 Tbsp. extra light olive oil or canola oil

4 boneless, skinless chicken breasts

½ tsp. salt

¼ tsp. ground black pepper

⅓ cup almonds, finely chopped

¼ cup shallots or green onions, minced

⅓ cup chicken broth

⅓ cup Welch's® Strawberry Spread

3 Tbsp. balsamic vinegar

1 Tbsp. fresh rosemary, minced (or 1 tsp. dried rosemary, crumbled)

1 bag fresh spinach (10 oz.), cooked until tender and warm

Fresh parsley, finely chopped (optional)

1. Heat a large nonstick skillet; add oil and heat over medium-high heat.

2. Sprinkle chicken with salt and pepper, dredge in almonds.

3. Place chicken in skillet; sauté 4 minutes on each side, turning once. Remove from pan and keep warm.

4. Reduce heat to low; add green onions to skillet and sauté 1 minute.

5. Add chicken broth, Welch's® Strawberry Spread, vinegar, and rosemary; simmer until slightly thickened, about 2 to 3 minutes.

6. Place spinach on heated serving platter; top with chicken breasts.

7. Pour sauce over top.

8. If desired, sprinkle finely chopped parsley over chicken.

Pork Roast with Grape-Apple Stuffing

1 pork loin (about 5 lbs.)

Salt to taste

Garlic powder to taste

1 package (8 oz.) stuffing mix

1 egg, well beaten

1 can (10½ oz.) condensed chicken broth

⅓ cup Welch's® Grape Jam

2 Tbsp. onion, minced

1 red apple, peeled, cored, and diced

1. Preheat oven to 350°F.

2. With sharp knife, cut along the rib of the pork loin, leaving 1-inch of uncut meat at each end. Cut almost to the bottom of the roast, forming a deep pocket.

3. Rub outside of meat and inside of pocket with salt and garlic powder.

4. Combine remaining ingredients and toss until blended.

5. Open pocket and stuff.

6. Place pork loin in a shallow pan on rack and roast for 2 to 2½ hours or internal temperature reaches 170°F. If stuffing becomes too brown, cover with foil.

7. Bake any remaining stuffing in a separate pan, covered, for 30 minutes.

Sweet & Sour Cabbage

6 servings

8 strips bacon, diced

1 medium head cabbage, shredded

2 tart apples, peeled, cored, and diced

¼ cup plus 1 Tbsp. cider vinegar

½ cup Welch's® Grape Jelly

Salt to taste

6 strips bacon, diced

1 medium head cabbage, shredded

2 tart apples, peeled, cored, and diced

¼ cup vinegar

½ cup Welch's® Grape Jelly

1. In a skillet, fry bacon until crisp. Remove and drain on paper towels.

2. Add cabbage, apples, ¼ cup vinegar, and Welch's® Grape Jelly to bacon drippings.

3. Cover and simmer over low heat for 30 to 40 minutes, until cabbage is tender.

4. Season to taste with salt and add 1 tablespoon venegar. Garnish with bacon.

Sauerbraten

1 pot roast (about 5 lbs.)

1 tsp. salt

2 Tbsp. vegetable oil

1 cup cider vinegar

2 cups water

1 cup dry red wine

1 cup onion, chopped

3 Tbsp. mixed whole pickling spice

3 Tbsp. all-purpose flour

⅓ cup Welch's® Grape Jelly

1 cup sour cream

1. Rub pot roast with salt.

2. In heavy Dutch oven, heat oil. Add pot roast and brown on all sides.

3. Stir in vinegar, water, wine, onion, and pickling spice.

4. Cover and simmer for $1\frac{1}{2}$ to 2 hours or until meat is tender.

5. Strain pan drippings and stir in flour. Add Welch's® Grape Jelly.

6. Cook over low heat, stirring constantly, until sauce thickens.

7. Stir in sour cream. Reheat but do not boil.

8. Cut meat into slices and serve with sauce.

Glazed Ham

4–6 servings

1 smoked ham (about 10 lbs.)

1 cup Welch's® Grape Juice

½ cup Welch's® Grape Jam

1 tsp. orange zest, grated

Pineapple for garnish, either fresh or canned

1. Combine Welch's® Grape Juice, Welch's® Grape Jam, and orange zest in a bowl and stir until blended.

2. Bake ham according to directions.

3. One hour before it is ready to be served, remove ham from oven. Using a sharp knife, score fat into diamonds.

4. Brush ham thickly with half of the glaze and return to oven. Bake 30 minutes, then brush with remaining glaze.

5. Cut fresh or canned pineapple into thick slices for garnish.

6. Place around the outside top of ham after it is removed from oven. Brush any remaining glaze over fruit.

Crispy Shrimp Dippers

4 servings

2 lbs. jumbo shrimp, shelled and deveined

1 cup all-purpose flour

1 egg, well beaten

¾ tsp. salt

1 cup beer or water

Vegetable oil, 1½-inch deep

1 cup Welch's® Grape Jelly

1 Tbsp. prepared horseradish

1 tsp. dry mustard

1. Wash shrimp and drain.

2. In a bowl, combine flour, egg, salt, and beer.

3. Beat with electric mixer until smooth. Add more beer, if necessary, until batter is the consistency of heavy cream.

4. Dip shrimp in batter and fry in oil until brown on both sides. Drain on paper towels.

5. Combine remaining ingredients and heat until bubbly.

6. Dip fried shrimp into sauce.

Tip:

Serve with hot cooked rice.

PBJ Banana Treats

2 Tbsp. peanut butter

2 hot dog buns

2 bananas

Welch's® Squeezable Grape Jelly

1 Tbsp raisins (optional)

1. Spread 1 tablespoon peanut butter onto each hot dog bun.

2. Place a banana in each bun.

3. Squeeze Welch's® Grape Jelly over the banana from the squeeze bottle. Sprinkle with raisins if desired.

Sticky Pizza

8 servings

1 (9-in.) refrigerated piecrust

½ cup peanut butter

⅓ cup Welch's® Grape Jam or Welch's® Grape Jelly

Butter, melted

Granulated sugar, to taste

Mini marshmallows

1. Preheat oven to 425°F.

2. On a baking sheet, arrange piecrust. Pinch edge of crust to form a ridge. Prick many holes in crust with a fork. If desired, brush edges with melted butter; sprinkle with sugar.

3. Bake 10 minutes or until golden brown; let cool slightly.

4. Evenly spread peanut butter on crust.

5. Cover peanut butter with Welch's® Grape Jam or Welch's® Grape Jelly.

6. Garnish with mini marshmallows. Cut into wedges.

Strawberry-filled Powdered Doughnuts

18 servings

2 envelopes dry yeast	1 tsp. salt	2 cups confectioners sugar
¼ cup warm water	2 eggs	1½ tsp. vanilla extract
1½ cups milk	5 cups all-purpose flour	4 Tbsp. hot water
⅔ cup unsalted butter	Vegetable oil for frying	
½ cup granulated sugar	Welch's® Strawberry Spread	

1. Sprinkle yeast over ¼ cup of warm water. Let stand until foamy.

2. In a saucepan, heat milk and ⅓ cup butter until most of the butter is melted.

3. In a mixing bowl, mix milk and butter mixture, sugar, salt, eggs, and 2 cups flour. Beat for a few minutes until well combined. Add softened yeast and stir into dough.

4. Beat in remaining flour, ½ cup at a time, until dough no longer sticks to bowl sides.

5. Knead about 5 minutes or until smooth and elastic. Place dough in a slightly greased bowl and cover with a towel. Set in a warm place to rise until doubled in size.

6. Turn dough out onto a floured surface and roll out to ½-inch thick. Cut with a floured round cookie or biscuit cutter.

7. Cover loosely with a towel and let rise again until doubled in size. While waiting for dough to rise, make Glaze.

8. Heat oil in a deep fryer or skillet to 350˚F. Fry doughnuts on each side until golden brown. Remove from oil and drain on a wire rack.

9. Dip warm doughnut into glaze, place on wire rack set over a cookie sheet or parchment or wax paper to drain excess glaze.

10. Using a piping tool, pipe about 1 teaspoon of Welch's® Strawberry Spread into center of each doughnut.

Glaze:

1. Melt butter in a saucepan. Stir in confectioners sugar and vanilla; stir until smooth.

2. Remove from heat. Add water one tablespoon at a time.
   Icing should be thin but not watery.

Quick Raisin Fingers

20–24 servings

1 loaf raisin bread

Butter, softened

¼ cup Welch's® Grape Jam

¾ cup flaked coconut

1. Trim crusts from slices of raisin bread. Cut each slice in half.

2. Toast bread slices and spread butter on one side.

3. Spread the buttered side of each piece of bread with Welch's® Grape Jam and sprinkle with coconut.

4. Return to broiler and broil until coconut is golden brown. Serve warm.

Grape Crunchies

36 servings

1½ cups raisins, chopped or coarsely ground

1½ cups corn flakes, slightly crushed

½ cup peanut butter

½ cup Welch's® Grape Jam

Peanuts, finely chopped

1. In a mixing bowl, combine raisins, corn flakes, peanut butter, and Welch's® Grape Jam. Stir until well blended.

2. Shape into balls; roll in chopped peanuts and chill until ready to serve.

Whirligigs

2 Tbsp. peanut butter

2 Tbsp. Welch's® Grape Jelly

Flatbread or tortilla

1. Spread peanut butter and Welch's®
   Grape Jelly on bread or tortilla.

2. Roll into a tight spiral. Cut each spiral
   into several pieces. Repeat to create
   additional pieces.

Cookies & Such

Chapter 5

Jam-Shortbread Cookies

4 cookies

1 cup unsalted butter, cut into tablespoon-sized pieces, room temperature

½ cup granulated sugar

1 tsp. vanilla extract

2½ cups all-purpose flour

1 cup Welch's® Grape Jam or Welch's® Grape Jelly

1. Preheat oven to 325°F. Line baking tray with parchment.
2. Beat butter with electric mixer on medium-high speed until creamy, about 5 minutes.
3. Gradually add sugar and continue beating on high speed until very light and fluffy; the mixture should be almost white in color. Beat in vanilla.
4. Beat in flour in three additions, mixing until dough has come together, scraping down bowl once or twice.
5. Roll out on floured surface to ⅛-inch thickness.
6. Cut out cookies using a 1¼-inch fluted edge round cookie cutter (or cookie cutter of your choice).
7. Transfer to prepared cookie sheet spacing cookies 1-inch apart. Refrigerate for 1 hour or overnight, if desired.
8. Bake about 10 to 12 minutes or until edges turn very light golden brown. The tops of the cookies should remain as white as possible.
9. Slide parchment onto cooling racks and cool cookies completely.
10. Spread a bit of Welch's® Grape Jam or Welch's® Grape Jelly on the bottom of a cookie and sandwich with another cookie.

Tip:

Cookies may be stored at room temperature in an airtight container for up to two weeks.

Cookie Rounds

Aproximately 8 cookies
Aproximately 8 cookies

1 cup butter

2½ cups all-purpose flour

1 cup small curd cottage cheese

¼ cup walnuts, finely chopped

Welch's® Grape Jelly

Confectioners sugar

1. Preheat oven to 375°F.

2. In a bowl, cut butter into flour with pastry blender until mixture becomes consistency of coarse meal.

3. Add cottage cheese and nuts. Mix until thoroughly blended.

4. Roll out on a lightly floured board to ⅛-inch thickness.

5. Cut dough into 2-inch circles. Cut a 1-inch circle out of the center of half of the cookies.

6. Place circles with hole in middle on top of whole circles. Press together lightly.

7. Bake on ungreased baking sheet for about 15 to 20 minutes, or until lightly browned. Cool.

8. Fill center of cookies with Welch's® Grape Jelly and dust with confectioners sugar.

Variation:

Top with chopped pistachios, walnuts, coconut, or toasted slivered almonds.

Jelly-kissed Peanut Butter Cookies

Approximately 30 cookies

¾ cups all-purpose flour

¾ tsp. salt

½ tsp. baking soda

⅓ cup creamy peanut butter

¼ cup unsalted butter, softened

⅓ cup brown sugar, firmly packed

1 large egg

½ tsp. vanilla extract

⅓ cup granulated sugar

3 tsp. Welch's® Grape Jelly

1. Preheat oven to 350°F.

2. In a bowl, sift together flour, salt, and baking soda.

3. In another bowl, cream together peanut butter, butter, and brown sugar until smooth. Add egg and vanilla; blend well.

4. Add flour to peanut butter mixture, stirring until blended.

5. Roll pieces of dough into 1-inch balls and roll in granulated sugar.

6. On a large baking sheet, arrange balls 2-inches apart and bake on middle oven rack for 10 minutes.

7. Working quickly, make an indentation with the back of a ¼ teaspoon of about 2-inches in diameter in the center of each cookie.

8. Fill each indentation with a slightly heaping teaspoon of Welch's® Grape Jelly and bake cookies for another 10 minutes or until golden brown. Transfer cookies to racks to cool.

Strawberry Nut Slices

1 cup butter

1 cup granulated sugar

3 egg yolks

2 cups all-purpose flour

1 cup pecans, chopped

½ cup Welch's® Strawberry Spread

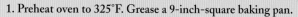

1. Preheat oven to 325°F. Grease a 9-inch-square baking pan.

2. Beat margarine and sugar until light and fluffy. Blend in egg yolks.

3. Add flour and nuts; mix well.

4. Spread half of dough onto bottom of baking pan; top with Welch's® Strawberry Spread, then with remaining dough mixture.

5. Bake 50 minutes or until lightly browned.

6. Cool; cut into squares.

Fruity Thumb Prints

36–48 servings

½ cup butter

⅓ cup granulated sugar

1 egg yolk

¼ tsp. vanilla

1¼ cups all-purpose flour

½ tsp. salt

1 egg white, slightly beaten

1 cup flaked coconut

Welch's® Grape Jam

1. Preheat oven to 300°F.

2. Cream butter. Gradually add sugar, beating until light and fluffy. Add egg yolk and vanilla.

3. Sift together flour and salt; add gradually to creamed mixture.

4. Chill dough. Shape into 1-inch balls. Dip in egg white, then roll in coconut.

5. Place on a lightly greased cookie sheet. Press top of each ball with thumb to form an indentation.

6. Bake 25 to 30 minutes, until lightly browned.

7. Cool and fill the indentation with Welch's® Grape Jam.

Jelly Surprise Cookies

Approximately 6 cookies

1 cup butter, softened

1½ cups granulated sugar

1 egg

1½ tsp. vanilla extract

3½ cups all-purpose flour

1 tsp. salt

1 tsp. baking soda

2 Tbsp. milk

¾ cup Welch's® Grape Jelly

1. Preheat oven to 350°F. Lightly grease baking sheets.

2. In a large bowl, cream butter, then add sugar until well mixed.

3. Add egg and vanilla; beat well.

4. Stir in flour, salt and soda; mix well. Add milk. Stir to make smooth dough.

5. Refrigerate for about 2 hours.

6. On a lightly floured board, roll out half the dough to ⅛-inch thickness.

7. Cut with a 2½-inch cookie cutter. Roll out remaining dough; cut with a 2½-inch cutter with a hole in the middle.

8. Place on baking sheets. Bake 8 to 10 minutes, or until lightly browned.

9. Cool for 30 minutes.

10. Spread Welch's® Grape Jelly on plain cookie; place cookies with hole on top.

Party Cookies

48 bakery cookies
(sugar, coconut, or lemon)

Welch's® Grape Jelly

Almond slivers

1. Spread half of the cookies with Welch's® Grape Jelly.

2. Sandwich plain cookies with jelly-coated cookies.

3. Decorate each sandwich with a stripe of Welch's® Grape Jelly across the top.

4. Scatter almond slivers over the stripes.

Pecan Jammers

8 cookies

⅔ cup pecan halves, lightly toasted and cooled

2 cups confectioners sugar, divided

¼ tsp. salt

1 cup unsalted butter, at room temperature, cut into tablespoon-sized pieces

1½ tsp. vanilla extract

2 cups all-purpose flour

¼ to ⅓ cup Welch's Grape Jam® or Welch's® Grape Jelly

Toasting pecans:

1. Preheat oven to 400°F.

2. Spread pecan halves on cookie sheet.

3. Bake 5 minutes. Shake pecans to ensure even toasting.

4. Bake 2 more minutes or until lightly browned. Let cool before adding to dough.

Cookies:

1. Preheat oven to 350°F. Line two rimmed jellyroll pans with parchment paper.

2. Place pecans, ½ cup confectioners sugar, and salt in bowl or food processor fitted with metal blade. Process until nuts are finely ground.

3. Add butter a few pieces at a time, then process until mixture is smooth; add vanilla.

4. Add flour and pulse machine on and off until incorporated, scraping the dough down once or twice.

5. Mix until the dough begins to form a ball.

6. Remove dough and form into a very flat disk; wrap in plastic wrap and refrigerate for at least 2 hours or until firm enough to roll into balls.

Tip:

Dough can be frozen up to one month before using; defrost in refrigerator overnight before proceeding.

7. Roll dough between lightly floured palms into 1-inch balls and place on cookie sheet 2-inches apart.

8. Make an indentation with your thumb or forefinger in the center of each cookie to make a deep well going about three-quarters of the way into the cookie. If cracks form, simply press them together.

9. Bake about 13 to 15 minutes or until light golden brown on the bottoms and around the edges.

10. Place cookie sheets on cooling racks; sift remaining 1½ cups confectioners sugar over warm cookies.

11. Immediately fill indentations with Welch's Grape Jam® or Welch's® Grape Jelly and allow to cool completely. Cookies may be stored at room temperature in an airtight container for up to two weeks. Place wax paper between layers to prevent sticking.

Welch's® Grape Pinwheels

60 cookies

1 cup butter, softened

1 package (8 oz.) cream cheese, softened

Granulated sugar

2 tsp. vanilla extract

⅛ tsp. salt

2¾ cups all-purpose flour

½ cup Welch's® Grape Jam

½ cup walnuts, chopped

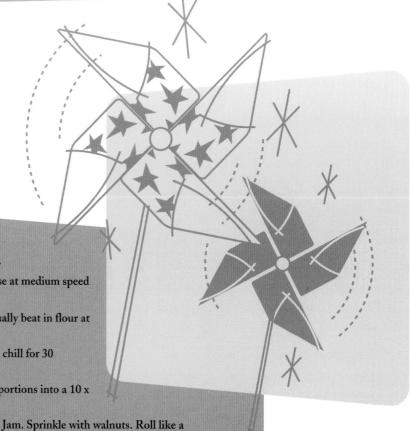

1. Preheat oven to 350°F. Grease cookie sheet.

2. In a large bowl, beat butter and cream cheese at medium speed until fluffy.

3. Beat in ½ cup sugar, vanilla, and salt. Gradually beat in flour at low speed, until a ball forms.

4. Divide dough into two portions. Cover and chill for 30 minutes.

5. On lightly floured surface, roll each dough portions into a 10 x 14-inch rectangle.

6. Spread each rectangle with Welch's® Grape Jam. Sprinkle with walnuts. Roll like a jellyroll, starting with 10-inch side.

7. Wrap in waxed paper and chill at least 4 hours.

8. Cut rolls into ½-inch slices. Dip one cut side in sugar. Place on cookie sheet, sugar side up.

9. Bake 25 to 30 minutes.

Concord Squares

About 60 squares

1 cup butter

1 package (8 oz.) cream cheese

2 cups all-purpose flour

½ tsp. baking powder

2 cups walnuts, finely chopped

1½ cups Welch's® Concord Grape Jam

2 tsp. granulated sugar

1. Preheat oven to 375°F.

2. In electric mixer bowl, cream butter and cream cheese.

3. Sift together flour and baking powder; add to creamed mixture. Mix until thoroughly blended.

4. Chill dough 2 to 3 hours.

5. Mix together nuts, Welch's® Concord Grape Jam, and sugar; set aside.

6. Divide dough into four equal parts. Work with one-fourth of the dough at a time. Refrigerate remaining dough.

7. Roll dough out on a lightly floured board to ⅛-inch thickness and cut into 2-inch squares.

8. Place half of the cookie squares on an ungreased baking sheet. Place 1 teaspoon nut mixture in center of each square and cover with remaining cookie squares. Pinch edges together with tines of a fork. Prick tops of each.

9. Bake 15 to 20 minutes.

Walnut Hearts with Jelly Jewels

1⅔ cups self-rising cake flour

2 Tbsp. granulated sugar

½ tsp. salt

⅓ cup walnuts, finely ground

¼ cup unsalted butter

1 egg

½ cup buttermilk

1 tsp. vanilla extract

All-purpose flour, for dusting

¼ cup Welch's® Grape Jelly

2 Tbsp. milk

Heart-shaped (about 3-in.) cookie cutter about 3-inch

1. Preheat oven to 350°F. Prepare baking sheet by buttering and flouring, or lining with parchment.

2. Sift flour, sugar, and salt in a mixing bowl.

3. Add ground walnuts.

4. Cut in butter until mixture resembles coarse meal.

5. In another bowl, whisk together egg, buttermilk, and vanilla.

6. Combine the wet and dry ingredients until just mixed. Be careful not to over mix.

7. Roll dough gently on a lightly floured surface.

8. With a heart-shaped cookie cutter, cut scones, reforming dough scraps and gently rolling and cutting until all dough is used.

9. Transfer scones to baking sheet.

10. With your thumb or the back of a teaspoon, press a shallow indent into the center of each heart.

11. Brush milk onto hearts and bake 10 to 12 minutes. Cool on baking rack.

12. Fill indentations with Welch's® Grape Jelly.

Spooky Spiderwebs

8 cookies

1 roll (16 oz.) refrigerated sugar cookie dough

¾ cup all-purpose flour

1 jar (12 oz.) Welch's® Grape Jam

1 tube black cake decorating gel

1. Preheat oven to 375°F. Prepare baking sheet with nonstick cooking spray, or parchment.

2. Unwrap cookie dough and place in a medium mixing bowl.

3. With floured hands, knead flour into cookie dough.

4. Roll dough back into log shape, place on clean cutting board and cut into 1-inch slices.

5. With floured fingers, place dough circles on baking sheet.

6. Gently press dough circles, flattening to make each one approximately 4-inches in diameter.

7. With thumb and forefinger, pinch the edge of each dough circle to create a ridge all around, making eight points.

8. Refrigerate for 20 minutes.

9. Bake 12 to 14 minutes or until edges are lightly browned.

10. Remove cookies from baking sheet and cool on wire rack.

11. Spread 2 tablespoons Welch's® Grape Jam onto each cookie, making sure to spread it all the way to the edges and into the points.

12. When cool, use the black decorating gel to make a spiderweb design.

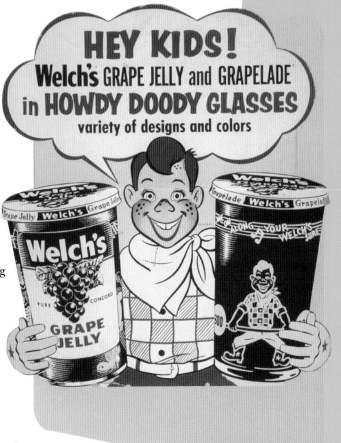

HEY KIDS!
Welch's GRAPE JELLY and GRAPELADE in HOWDY DOODY GLASSES
variety of designs and colors

PBJ Layer Cookies

6 cookies

1½ cups all-purpose flour

½ cup plus 1 Tbsp. granulated sugar

½ tsp. baking soda

¼ tsp. salt

½ cup creamy peanut butter

½ cup butter-flavored vegetable shortening

3 Tbsp. milk

1 egg yolk

1 tsp. vanilla extract

Welch's® Grape Jelly

Granulated sugar

1. Preheat oven to 350°F.

2. Combine flour, sugar, baking soda, and salt in a large bowl.

3. Cut in peanut butter and shortening into dry ingredients using pastry blender, or two knives, until mixture resembles coarse meal.

4. Combine milk, egg yolk, and vanilla in a small bowl. Beat with fork until blended.

5. Add to flour mixture. Beat with electric mixer at low speed until well blended.

6. Divide dough in half. Wrap with plastic wrap and refrigerate for at least 1 hour.

7. Roll each half of dough between sheets of plastic wrap to ⅛-inch thickness.

8. Cut with 2½-inch cookie cutters.

9. Place half the cutouts 1-inch apart on ungreased baking sheets.

10. Place about ½ teaspoon Welch's® Grape Jelly in center of each. Top with remaining cutouts.

11. Press edges with fork and prick top several times with toothpick.

12. Sprinkle cookies lightly with sugar. Bake 10 to 11 minutes, or until golden brown.

13. Sprinkle again with sugar.

14. Cool on baking sheet 5 minutes. Remove cookies from pans to cool completely.

Grape Bars

48 bars

1¾ cups all-purpose flour

½ tsp. baking soda

½ tsp. salt

1½ cups rolled oats

1 cup butter

1 cup brown sugar, firmly packed

1 cup Welch's® Grape Jam

½ cup pecans, finely chopped (optional)

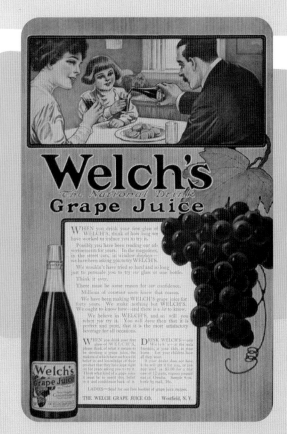

1. Preheat oven to 400°F.

2. Mix flour, soda, and salt; add oats and mix.

3. Cream butter. Add sugar gradually; cream until fluffy. Add the flour mixture.

4. Reserve one-fourth of crumbs for topping. Firmly press remainder in a greased 13 x 9 x 2-inch pan.

5. Spread Welch's® Grape Jam carefully over layer in pan.

6. Sprinkle with reserved topping and chopped nuts.

7. Bake in oven for about 25 minutes.

Strawberry-Oatmeal Bars

12 bars

1 cup all-purpose flour

1 cup rolled oats

½ cup butter, softened

⅓ cup light brown sugar, firmly packed

¼ tsp. baking powder

⅛ tsp. salt

¾ cup Welch's® Strawberry Spread

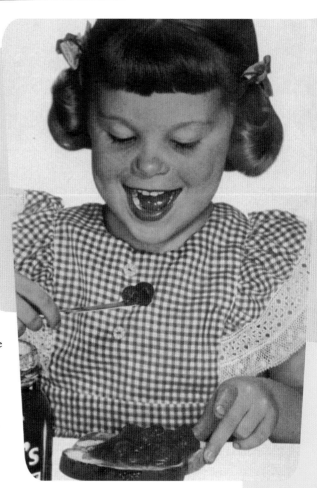

1. Preheat oven to 375°F.

2. In a large bowl, mix everything together except the Welch's® Strawberry Spread.

3. Measure out 2 cups of this mixture. Leave the rest in the bowl and set aside.

4. Take the 2 cups of the mixture and press it into the bottom of an 8-inch-square pan coated with nonstick spray. Using a large spoon, distribute Welch's® Strawberry Spread on top of the mixture in the pan. Spread it evenly all over.

5. Take the remaining mixture and spread it over the Welch's® Strawberry Spread. Press down lightly.

6. Bake 25 minutes.

7. Remove the pan from the oven and allow it to cool for at least 15 minutes. Cut into bars.

Welch's® Cookie Cheesecake Squares

12 squares

1 cup all-purpose flour

1 cup rolled oats

½ cup butter, softened

⅓ cup light brown sugar, firmly packed

¼ tsp. baking powder

⅛ tsp. salt

¾ cup Welch's® Strawberry Spread

1. Preheat oven to 375°F.

2. In a large bowl, mix everything together except the Welch's® Strawberry Spread.

3. Measure out 2 cups of this mixture. Leave the rest in the bowl and set aside.

4. Take the 2 cups of the mixture and press it into the bottom of an 8-inch-square pan coated with nonstick spray. Using a large spoon, distribute Welch's® Strawberry Spread on top of the mixture in the pan. Spread it evenly all over.

5. Take the remaining mixture and spread it over the Welch's® Strawberry Spread. Press down lightly.

6. Bake 25 minutes.

7. Remove the pan from the oven and allow it to cool for at least 15 minutes. Cut into bars.

Welch's® Grape Crumble Bars

36 bars

¾ cup butter

1 cup brown sugar, firmly packed

1½ cups all-purpose flour

1 tsp. salt

½ tsp. baking soda

2 cups ready-to-eat all-natural cereal or granola with raisins and dates

1 jar (10 oz.) Welch's® Grape Jelly

1. Preheat oven to 400°F.

2. Cream butter and sugar until light and fluffy.

3. Add flour, salt, and soda; mix well. Stir in cereal.

4. Press half the dough into a well-greased 13 x 9-inch pan.

5. Break up Welch's® Grape Jelly with a fork; spread over dough in pan, up to ⅛-inch from the edges.

6. With fingers, crumble the remaining dough over the top.

7. Bake about 20 minutes, or until brown. Cool; cut into bars.

Peanutty Jelly Bars

16 bars

1½ cups all-purpose flour

½ cup granulated sugar

¾ tsp. baking powder

½ cup cold butter

1 egg, beaten

¾ cup Welch's® Grape Jelly

1⅔ cup (10-oz. package) peanut butter chips, divided

1. Preheat oven to 375°F. Grease a 9-inch-square baking pan.

2. Stir together flour, sugar, and baking powder; cut in butter with pastry blender or fork until mixture resembles coarse crumbs. Stir in beaten egg until blended.

3. Reserve half of mixture; press remaining mixture into bottom of prepared pan.

4. Stir Welch's® Grape Jelly slightly; spread evenly over crust.

5. Sprinkle 1 cup peanut butter chips over Welch's® Grape Jelly.

6. Stir remaining ⅔ cup peanut butter chips into reserved crumb mixture; sprinkle over top.

7. Bake 25 to 30 minutes, or until lightly browned.

8. Cool completely in pan on wire rack. Cut into bars.

Grape-Coconut Bars

12 servings

1 cup all-purpose flour

1 tsp. baking powder

½ cup butter, chilled

2 eggs, beaten

1 Tbsp. water

1 cup Welch's® Grape Jelly

⅔ cup granulated sugar

¼ cup butter, melted

2 cups unsweetened coconut

¾ tsp. vanilla

1. Preheat oven to 350°F. Grease a 13 x 9-inch pan.

2. Mix together flour and baking powder in a medium bowl.

3. Cut in the butter until coarse crumbs form.

4. Stir in eggs and water.

5. Spread dough into prepared pan.

6. Spread Welch's® Grape Jelly over the top.

7. In medium bowl, combine sugar, melted butter, coconut, and vanilla.

8. Sprinkle evenly over top of jelly layer, gently pressing down.

9. Bake 30 minutes, or until coconut is lightly browned.

10. Let cool completely before cutting into bars.

Fabulous Finales

Chapter 6

Special Bread Pudding with Strawberries

9 servings

4 cups stale egg or white bread, cut into 1-inch squares

2½ cups strawberries, coarsely chopped

½ cup Welch's® Strawberry Spread

2 cups half-and-half

4 large eggs, lightly beaten

½ cup granulated sugar

1 Tbsp. vanilla extract

⅛ tsp. salt

⅛ cup prepared caramel or butterscotch sauce, warmed

Whipping cream, sweetened and whipped

Whole strawberries (optional)

1. Preheat oven to 375° F. Lightly coat a 9-inch-square baking pan with cooking spray; set aside.

2. In large bowl, combine bread, Welch's® Strawberry Spread, and chopped strawberries.

3. In medium bowl, whisk together half-and-half, eggs, sugar, vanilla, and salt until well blended; pour over bread mixture.

4. Let stand 10 minutes, pushing bread down into egg mixture occasionally.

5. Pour mixture into prepared pan.

6. Bake 50 to 55 minutes or until top is golden brown and knife inserted into center comes out clean.

7. Serve warm with caramel or butterscotch sauce, whipped cream, and whole strawberries, if desired.

Zebra Parfaits

4–5 servings

1½ cups Welch's® Grape Jelly

1 package vanilla pudding

1. Prepare pudding according to package directions. Refrigerate until firm.

2. Alternate layers of pudding and chilled Welch's® Grape Jelly in dessert dishes.

Revel Rice Pudding

1 package (5 oz.) instant rice

½ cup brown sugar

½ cup raisins

¼ cup light cream

¼ cup Welch's® Grape Jelly

1. In a saucepan, cook rice according to package directions.

2. Thoroughly combine hot rice, brown sugar, and raisins. Chill.

3. Whip cream and fold into rice.

4. Just before serving, swirl Welch's® Grape Jelly through rice mixture.

Old-Fashioned Jellyroll

8 servings

4 eggs, at room temperature

¾ cups all-purpose or cake flour

1 tsp. baking powder

¼ tsp. salt

¾ cup granulated sugar

1 tsp. vanilla extract or 1 Tbsp. orange zest, grated

Confectioners sugar

1 jar (10 oz.) Welch's® Grape Jelly

1. Preheat oven to 400°F. Line a 15 x 10½ x 1-inch jellyroll pan with greased waxed paper.

2. Sift together flour, baking powder, and salt; set aside.

3. With electric mixer, beat eggs at high speed until thick and lemon colored. Gradually beat in sugar, 2 tablespoons at a time, continuing to beat until very thick and light (about 5 minutes).

4. At low speed, blend in sifted dry ingredients and vanilla just until combined.

5. Spread evenly in jellyroll pan.

6. Bake about 10 to 13 minutes, until surface springs back when gently pressed with finger.

7. Sift confectioners sugar onto a clean towel at least 15 x 10-inches.

8. With sharp knife, loosen sides of cake from pan. Turn onto the sugared towel; gently peel off waxed paper and trim off crisp edges.

9. Starting with 10-inch side, roll cake in towel; place seam side down on wire rack until cool.

10. Gently unroll cake, remove towel and spread unpowdered side with Welch's® Grape Jelly. *Tip: Beat jelly with a fork for spreading consistency.*

11. Reroll and place seam side down on serving plate; cover loosely with foil.

12. Chill at least 1 hour. Top with sifted confectioners sugar.

Cream Cheese–Strawberry Turnovers

4 servings

1 package (8 oz.) refrigerated crescent dinner rolls

Confectioners sugar

⅓ cup whipped cream cheese

¼ cup Welch's® Strawberry Spread

1 egg white, beaten

1. Preheat oven to 375°F.

2. On cookie sheet, separate dough into 4 rectangles. Pinch seams closed.

3. Sprinkle with confectioners sugar.

4. Spoon 1 teaspoon each of the cream cheese and Welch's® Strawberry Spread in the center of each rectangle.

5. Brush edges with egg white. Fold in half and pinch edges with fork.

6. Brush tops with egg white.

7. Bake 15 to 20 minutes or until browned. Sprinkle with confectioners sugar.

Royal Cheesecake

12–14 servings

1½ cups graham cracker crumbs

2 Tbsp. granulated sugar

⅓ cup butter, melted

2 packages (8 oz. each) cream cheese

4 cups milk

¼ tsp. ground cinnamon

2 packages lemon instant pudding mix

1 jar (10 oz.) Welch's® Grape Jam

1. Preheat oven to 350°F.

2. In a bowl, combine graham cracker crumbs and sugar. Add melted butter; stir thoroughly to blend.

3. Pack mixture firmly into bottom, and about two-thirds up sides of a 9-inch spring-form pan.

4. Bake until lightly browned. Cool.

5. In a bowl, beat cream cheese until softened.

6. Add 1 cup milk, a little at a time, blending until mixture is smooth.

7. Add remaining milk, cinnamon, and pudding mix. Beat until well blended with an electric mixer.

8. Pour into crust and chill until set, about 2 hours.

9. Just before serving, spread jar of Welch's® Grape Jam over surface of cheesecake.

Jeweled Golden Cheesecake

6–8 servings

1 cup quick cooking oats

¼ cup peanuts, chopped

3 Tbsp. brown sugar, firmly packed

3 Tbsp. butter, softened

2 packages (8 oz. each) cream cheese, softened

1 cup granulated sugar

½ cup chunky peanut butter

3 Tbsp. all-purpose flour

4 eggs

½ cup milk

½ cup Welch's® Grape Jelly

1. Preheat oven to 325°F.

2. Combine oats, peanuts, brown sugar, and butter; press into bottom of 9-inch spring-form pan.

3. Bake 10 minutes and remove from oven. Increase oven temperature to 450°F.

4. Combine cream cheese, sugar, peanut butter, and flour, mixing at medium speed on electric mixer until well blended. *Note: Batter will be very stiff.*

5. Add eggs, one at a time, mixing well after each addition. Blend in milk.

6. Pour mixture over crust.

7. Bake 10 minutes. Reduce oven temperature to 250°F; continue baking for 30 to 35 minutes.

8. Loosen cake from rim of pan; cool before removing rim.

9. Heat Welch's® Grape Jelly until melted; spoon over cheesecake. Chill.

Tip:

Cooking the cheesecake in a water bath helps to avoid cracking in the latter stage of baking.

Swirly Bundt Cake

6–8 servings

2½ cups all-purpose flour

1½ tsp. baking powder

1 tsp. baking soda

½ tsp. salt

¾ cup unsalted butter, room temperature

1½ cups granulated sugar

¾ cup chunky peanut butter

2 tsp. vanilla extract.

3 large eggs

1 cup sour cream

½ cup Welch's® Grape Jelly

1. Preheat oven to 350°F. Place baking rack in bottom third of oven.

2. Whisk together flour, baking powder, baking soda, and salt; set aside.

3. In large bowl, beat butter and sugar together until light and fluffy.

4. Add peanut butter and vanilla, beating until well combined.

5. Add eggs, one at a time, beating until incorporated. Beat in sour cream.

6. Reduce mixer to lowest speed and gradually add flour mixture, mixing until just blended.

7. Spoon half of the batter (about 3 cups) into greased 12-cup bundt pan.

8. Dollop 3 tablespoons Welch's® Grape Jelly over batter, avoiding edges of pan. Partially stir jelly into batter using a skewer or thin bladed knife.

9. Spoon remaining batter into pan. Dollop and swirl remaining Welch's® Grape Jelly into batter.

10. Bake 50 to 60 minutes or until a wooden skewer inserted into center comes out clean.

11. Let cake cool in pan for 10 minutes, then invert onto wire rack. Serve warm or at room temperature.

Grapelade Cake

8–10 servings

3 cups all-purpose flour

1 tsp. baking powder

3 tsp. baking soda

¼ tsp. salt

1 tsp. ground cinnamon

1 tsp. ground cloves

⅔ cup butter

1½ cups granulated sugar

3 eggs, well beaten

1½ cups Welch's® Grape Jam

1 cup sour milk or buttermilk

Lavender Coconut

1 bag shredded coconut

Welch's® Concentrated Grape Juice, frozen

1. Preheat oven to 350°F. Grease and flour two 9 x 13-inch layer cake pans.

2. In a bowl, sift together flour, baking powder, soda, salt, and spices.

3. Cream shortening until soft and smooth. Gradually add sugar, continuing to beat until very fluffy.

4. Beat in eggs and Welch's® Grape Jam. Add flour mixture alternately with sour milk, mixing after each addition, until mixture is smooth.

5. Bake about 30 minutes.

6. Put layers together using butter or boiled frosting as filling. Frost cake on top with same icing.

7. Garnish with Lavender Coconut.

Lavender Coconut

1. Tint coconut with a few drops of Welch's® Concentrated Grape Juice, thawed and undiluted.

2. Mix with a spoon to blend

Strawberry-Citrus Loaf

8 servings

1 cup butter

1½ cups granulated sugar

4 eggs

1 cup Welch's® Strawberry Spread

3 cups all-purpose flour

¾ tsp. cream of tartar

½ tsp. baking soda

½ cup sour cream

1 tsp. vanilla extract

1 tsp. lemon juice

1 tsp. orange zest, grated

1. Preheat oven to 350°F. Grease two loaf pans.

2. Cream margarine and sugar. Add eggs one at a time, beating well.

3. Add Welch's® Strawberry Spread.

4. Mix in flour, cream of tartar, and baking soda.

5. Add sour cream, vanilla, lemon juice, and orange zest.

6. Pour into loaf pans and bake about 50 to 60 minutes, or until knife inserted comes out clean.

Concord Grape-Nut Bread

1 loaf

1 cup milk

1 egg

½ cup granulated sugar

1 Tbsp. butter or margarine, melted

2 cups all-purpose flour

½ tsp. salt

1 tsp. baking soda

1 tsp. baking powder

¼ cup walnuts, chopped

⅓ cup chopped candied fruits

⅓ cup Welch's® Concord Grape Jam

1. Preheat oven to 350°F. Grease and lightly flour a 9 x 5-inch loaf pan.

2. Combine milk, egg, sugar, and butter in a bowl, stirring briefly.

3. Mix dry ingredients and combine with liquids. Stir briefly. Add walnuts and candied fruits.

4. Pour ½ the batter into loaf pan. Pour Welch's® Concord Grape Jam over batter in a strip down the middle. Pour remaining batter over Welch's® Grape Jam.

5. Bake about 55 minutes, or until bread tests done.

6. Cool 15 minutes on wire rack before removing from pan.

Jam Twirls

16 servings

2 cups all-purpose flour

3 tsp. baking powder

1 tsp. salt

¼ cup butter

¾ cup milk

1 cup Welch's® Concord Grape Jam

¼ cup candied lemon zest, finely chopped

¼ cup nuts, finely chopped

Confectioners sugar

1. Preheat oven to 425°F.

2. In a bowl, combine flour, baking powder, and salt.

3. Cut in shortening until particles are very fine. Add milk and stir, until dough cleans the bowl.

4. Remove to a lightly floured board and knead a few times until smooth.

5. Roll out dough to a 12 x 16-inch rectangle.

6. Spread with Welch's® Concord Grape Jam and sprinkle with lemon zest and nuts. Roll up like a jellyroll, starting at the 16-inch side.

7. Cut roll into 16 1-inch slices. Place rolls side by side in a heavily buttered 9-inch square pan.

8. Bake 15 to 20 minutes, or until brown.

9. Remove from pan while hot. Serve warm, sprinkled with confectioners sugar.

Welch's **Grapelade**

a pure grape spread

Made from whole ripe "WELCH QUALITY" grapes without skins, seeds or grit-like crystals With bread, biscuits and as a sauce for meat. — Saves butter

Fluffy Grape Whip

6 servings

2 eggs, whole, plus 2 eggs divided

1 cup Welch's® Concord Grape Jam

¼ cup frozen Welch's® Grape Juice concentrate, thawed

1 Tbsp. lemon juice

1 envelope unflavored gelatin

¼ cup Welch's® Grape Juice, prepared

1 cup whipping cream, whipped

1. In top of double boiler, combine 2 whole eggs, 2 egg yolks (reserve whites), ½ cup Welch's® Concord Grape Jam, Welch's® Grape Juice concentrate, and lemon juice.

2. Cook and stir over simmering water until mixture thickens slightly, about two minutes. Remove from heat.

3. Soften gelatin in Welch's® Grape Juice; stir into cooked mixture to dissolve. Chill, stirring occasionally, until mixture just begins to set. (Don't let it setup or the mousse will be chunky.)

4. Beat reserved egg whites to form soft peaks. Fold into grape mixture with whipping cream.

5. Spoon into six individual dessert dishes; chill to set. Just before serving, warm remaining ½ cup Welch's® Grape Jam. Spoon a little over each serving.

Frozen Grape Custard

4 servings

2 eggs, well beaten

½ cup granulated sugar

¼ cup Welch's® Grape Juice

2 tsp. lemon zest, grated

Dash of salt

1 cup heavy whipping cream, whipped

½ cup Welch's® Grape Jelly

¼ cup almonds, chopped

1. In the top of a double boiler, combine eggs, sugar, Welch's® Grape Juice, and lemon zest. Put over hot (not boiling) water. Cook over low heat, stirring constantly, until mixture thickens or until custard coats a silver spoon*. Cool.

2. Add salt and fold in whipped cream; beat until mixture is smooth.

3. Fill parfait glasses half full with grape mixture; add two tablespoons Welch's® Grape Jelly to each.

4. Fill glasses to top with remainder of grape mixture. Sprinkle with almonds.

5. Cover with plastic wrap and freeze until firm, about 2 hours.

*If custard should start to curdle, beat vigorously at once with a whisk until smooth.

Grape Chill

6 servings

1 jar (10 oz.) Welch's® Grape Jelly

1 cup lemon juice

1½ cups granulated sugar

4 cups water

2 egg whites, beaten

2 navel oranges, peeled and sectioned

1. In a saucepan, mash Welch's® Grape Jelly; mix with lemon juice and sugar.

2. Place over low heat, stirring constantly, until sugar dissolves and Welch's® Grape Jelly melts.

3. Cool and stir in water. Freeze until half frozen.

4. Pour into a bowl and beat until fluffy. Fold in egg whites.

5. Pour into freezer tray, cover, and freeze until firm.

6. Spoon into six sherbet glasses; garnish with orange sections.

Variation:

Top with coconut, chopped walnuts or pecans, marshmallow fluff, or whipped cream.

Welch SHERBET

Recipe

1½ pints **Welch's**
1 quart water
1½ lbs. sugar.
Juice of 2 lemons.

When nearly frozen add beaten whites of two eggs to which powdered sugar has been added continue freezing several minutes.

Vineyard Haven Wedding Cake

40–45 servings

5 packages (18 oz. each) yellow cake mix

Grated zest of 5 oranges

2 Tbsp. nutmeg

10 eggs

6½ cups water

2½ cups Welch's® Grape Jelly

5 cans (16 oz. each) vanilla frosting

Small clusters red, green, and purple grapes

1 egg white, slightly beaten

Granulated sugar

Wedding ornament

1. Pour cake mixes into very large bowl. Add grated rind, nutmeg, eggs, and water. Beat with electric hand mixer until well blended and smooth.

2. Pour batter into greased and floured layer cake pans: two 11-inch pans, two 9-inch pans, and two 7-inch pans. Fill pans about half full.

3. Bake 11-inch pans for about 40 to 45 minutes, 9-inch pans for about 30 to 35 minutes, and 7-inch pans for about 30 minutes. Turn layers out on rack and cool.

4. Place 11-inch layer on large serving platter. Trim top to make it flat.

5. Spread first layer with some of the Welch's® Grape Jelly and top with second 11-inch layer. Trim layer to make it flat.

6. Spread Welch's® Grape Jelly in a 9-inch round on top of cake and add a 9-inch layer. Repeat, ending with a plain 7-inch layer.

7. Frost the top and sides of cake.

8. Fill a star-tipped pastry bag with remaining frosting and decorate cake with rosettes and scallops.

9. Wash grape clusters well, then dry.

10. Dip grapes into beaten egg white. Roll in granulated sugar. Dry at room temperature.

11. Place grapes in attractive arrangement, cascading down the front of the cake, using wooden skewers to hold bunches in place.

12. Top cake with wedding ornament.

Lemon Chiffon Pie

3 egg yolks, slightly beaten

1½ cups Welch's® Grape Juice

½ cup granulated sugar

1 package (3 oz.) lemon-flavored gelatin

2 Tbsp. lemon juice

1 tsp. lemon zest, grated

3 egg whites

Dash of salt

1 (9-in.) graham cracker crust

Welch's Grape Jelly

1. In a saucepan, mix egg yolks, 1 cup Welch's® Grape Juice, and ¼ cup sugar.

2. Cook over low heat, stirring constantly, just to a boil. Remove from heat; add gelatin and stir until dissolved.

3. Add remainder of Welch's® Grape Juice, lemon juice, and zest; chill until slightly thickened.

4. Beat egg whites and salt until foamy. Add remaining ¼ cup sugar, a little at a time, beating after each addition until blended.

5. Continue beating until mixture stands in stiff peaks.

6. Beat gelatin mixture slightly; gently fold in egg whites. Pour into graham cracker crust.

7. Chill several hours. Garnish with spoonfuls of Welch's® Grape Juice.

Elegant Trifle

8–10 servings

4 egg yolks

½ cup granulated sugar

2 tsp. vanilla extract

1 cup milk

1 cup light cream

2 sponge cake layers

½ cup sherry

1 cup Welch's® Grape Jam

⅓ cup shelled almonds

1 cup heavy cream

1 Tbsp. granulated sugar

1. In the top of a double boiler, beat egg yolks with sugar until well blended. Add vanilla.

2. Stir in milk and light cream.

3. Place over boiling water and cook, stirring constantly for about 15 minutes, until custard is thick enough to coat a wooden spoon.

4. Chill several hours, covered with plastic wrap touching custard to keep a film from developing.

5. Meanwhile, place a layer of sponge cake in a large crystal bowl.

6. Pour one-half the sherry over the cake; spread with ½ cup Welch's® Grape Jam.

7. Stud cake layer with one-half of the almonds.

8. Repeat Steps 5–7 with remaining layer. Top first layer with second layer. Refrigerate until ready to serve.

9. Combine heavy cream and remaining sugar; beat until stiff.

10. Just before serving, pour custard over cake layers.

11. Top with whipped cream. Garnish with additional almonds.

Special Occasions
Chapter 7

Candied Nut Mix

3½ cups

1 tsp. vegetable oil

4 cups salted mixed nuts

1½ cups Welch's® Strawberry Spread

2 Tbsp. paprika

2 tsp. cumin

Coating

½ cup brown sugar

1 tsp. paprika

1 tsp. cumin

1. Mix brown sugar coating ingredients together. Set aside.

2. Lightly oil a large stainless steel bowl. Place nuts in bowl. Set aside.

3. In a small saucepan, melt Welch's® Strawberry Spread over medium heat. Add paprika and cumin.

4. Cook the mixture to the softball or firmball stage, 230°F to 240°F on a candy thermometer*.

5. Immediately pour the mixture over the nuts.

6. Stir with a wooden spoon to evenly coat the nut mixture.

7. Cool for 5 minutes. Once cool enough to handle, sprinkle nuts with the brown sugar coating. Stir to combine.

8. Let cool completely, then pack into decorative, airtight tins.

Test for the stage by dropping a teaspoon of the mixture into a glass of iced water. The mixture retain its shape when ready.

Holiday Punch

Juice of 2 lemons

Juice of 2 limes

2 Tbsp. fresh ginger, chopped, or ½ tsp. ground ginger

1 cup Welch's® Strawberry Spread

4 cups cranberry juice

4 cups seltzer water

Lemon or lime slices, if desired

1. Combine lemon juice, lime juice, ginger, and Welch's® Strawberry Spread in a small saucepan or microwaveable bowl.

2. Heat mixture over medium heat and simmer for 5 minutes, stirring twice to help Welch's® Strawberry Spread dissolve*. Cool.

3. Combine cooled mixture, cranberry juice, and seltzer.

4. Pour over crushed ice; garnish drinks with lemon and lime slices.

*Microwave directions: Heat ingredients from step one in microwave-safe bowl, on high, for 2 minutes, until Welch's® Strawberry Spread dissolves.

Pineapple-Chicken Kabobs

4 servings of 2 kabobs each

16 (1-in.) chunks fresh pineapple

1½ lbs. skinless, boneless chicken breasts or thighs,
cut into 24 (1-in) pieces

Nonstick cooking spray

Sweet and Sour Sauce

½ cup Welch's® Grape Jelly

2 Tbsp soy sauce

1 Tbsp Worcestershire sauce

½ cup cider vinegar

1. In a small saucepan, combine ingredients for sweet and sour sauce.

2. Simmer over medium heat for 5 minutes, stirring constantly. Set aside.

3. Assemble kabobs, alternating chicken and pineapple, so each skewer has three chicken pieces and two pineapple chunks.

4. Lightly spray each kabob with nonstick cooking spray.

5. Grill or broil kabobs until chicken is cooked through.

6. Brush kabobs with sweet and sour sauce.

7. Serve with extra sauce for dipping.

Hot Wings with Strawberry Sauce

6 servings

Wings

½ cup apricot preserves

1 Tbsp. vinegar

1 to 2 tsp. hot pepper sauce

½ tsp. chili powder

½ large clove garlic, minced

2 lb. chicken wings

Sauce

½ cup Welch's® Strawberry Spread

1 package (3 oz.) cream cheese

½ cup sour cream

1 rounded Tbsp. onion soup mix

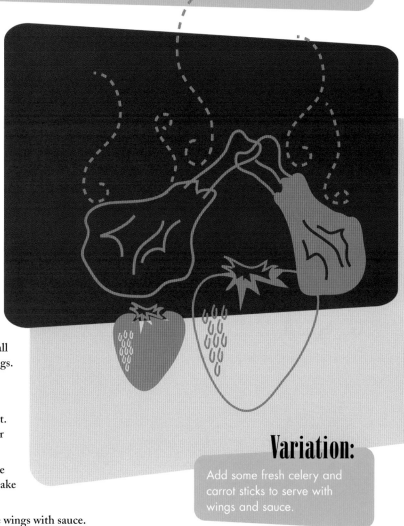

1. Preheat oven to 350°F.

2. In a medium mixing bowl, stir together all wings ingredients except for chicken wings.

3. On a clean cutting board, using a sharp knife, cut off tips of wings and discard.

4. Cut each chicken wing in half at the joint. Add wings to ingredients in bowl and stir to coat.

5. Place wings in large baking dish and bake 30 minutes. Turn up heat to 400°F and bake 15 minutes longer.

6. Mix together all sauce ingredients. Serve wings with sauce.

Variation:

Add some fresh celery and carrot sticks to serve with wings and sauce.

Sweet & Sour Meatballs

6–8 servings

Meatballs

2 lbs. ground beef

2 eggs, slightly beaten

1 cup dry bread crumbs

2 Tbsp. parsley flakes

1 onion, chopped

2 tsp. salt

2 Tbsp. Worcestershire sauce

½ tsp. ground black pepper

Sauce

1 bottle (12 oz.) chili sauce

1 Tbsp lemon juice

1 jar (10 oz.) Welch's® Grape Jelly

1 Tbsp. soy sauce

2 Tbsp. brown sugar, firmly packed

1. Mix ground beef with other meatball ingredients.

2. Shape into balls. Brown and drain.

3. Mix sauce ingredients well.

4. Drop meatballs into sauce.

5. Simmer for 45 minutes, uncovered.

Spicy Mini-Dogs

8 servings

2 bottles (12 oz. each) chili sauce

1 jar (8 oz.) Welch's® Grape Jelly

2 packages hot dogs, sliced into ¾ to 1-inch pieces (bite-sized hot dogs can also be used)

1. Heat chili sauce in medium saucepan until simmering.

2. Blend in Welch's® Grape Jelly and stir in hot dog slices.

3. Simmer on low heat for 20 minutes. Serve warm on toothpicks.

Variation:

Hot dogs can also be prepared in a crock pot.

Wrap & Roll Bites

20 servings

1 package egg roll wrappers

Peanut butter

Welch's® Grape Jelly

Water to seal wrapper edges

Deep fryer or 2-inch-deep vegetable oil

1. Fill each wrapper with 1 tablespoon peanut butter and 1 tablespoon Welch's® Grape Jelly.

2. Roll sides up and seal with a little water.

3. Deep fry until rolls bubble and turn brown. Serve warm.

Fruit Salad Delight

4 servings

2 small cantaloupes, halved and seeded

1 pint strawberries, stemmed

1 cup pineapple or lemon sherbet

½ cup Welch's® Strawberry Spread

¼ cup orange juice

Mint sprigs (optional)

1. Remove fruit from melons with melon baller.

2. Arrange melon balls and strawberries in melon halves.

3. Top each with scoops of sherbet.

4. Mix Welch's® Strawberry Spread and orange juice; spoon over sherbet.

5. Garnish with mint sprigs, if desired.

Red Grape Dessert Fondues

2⅔ cups fondue

2 cups Welch's® Red Grape Juice

5 Tbsp. cornstarch

1 cup Welch's® Grape Jelly

2 Tbsp. brandy (optional)

1. In a saucepan, gradually stir some of the Welch's® Red Grape Juice into the cornstarch until smooth.

2. Add remaining Welch's® Red Grape Juice and Welch's® Grape Jelly.

3. Cook and stir over medium heat, until fondue mixture comes to a boil and thickens.

4. Continue stirring. Cook gently for 1 to 2 minutes.

5. Stir in brandy if desired.

6. Transfer to fondue pot and keep warm while serving.

Fruit & Jam Dip

2½ cups

2 cups Welch's® Grape Jam

½ cup dry red wine

3 tsp. orange zest, grated

¼ tsp. ground cinnamon

¼ tsp. ground nutmeg

⅛ tsp. ground cloves

1. Combine all ingredients and pour into serving bowl. Chill.

2. Serve with crackers, crisp apple slices, pineapple spears, and orange sections.

Grape Napoleons

1 package (4 oz.) lemon pudding and pie filling

2½ cups Welch's® Concord Grape Juice

¼ cup granulated sugar

2 egg yolks, slightly beaten

1 tsp. lemon zest, grated

1 package piecrust mix

½ cup heavy cream, whipped

¾ cup confectioners sugar

2 Tbsp. water

2 Tbsp. Welch's® Concord Grape Jam

1. Preheat oven to 425°F.

2. In a saucepan, empty contents of pie filling package.

3. Gradually add Welch's® Concord Grape Juice, sugar, egg yolks, and lemon zest, stirring until mixture is smooth.

4. Cook directly over medium heat, stirring constantly, for about 5 minutes, until mixture starts to boil.

5. Remove from heat; cover surface with wax paper and chill.

6. Make piecrust as directed. Roll piecrust dough into a 10 x 14-inch rectangle.

7. Cut three equal length strips, about 3⅓ x 14-inch, and place on baking sheet.

8. Prick well with fork and bake about 12 minutes, until golden brown.

9. Beat chilled pie filling until light and fluffy; blend in whipped cream.

10. Spread two of the pastry strips with pie filling; stack all three strips one on top of another.

11. Combine confectioners sugar and water; stir until smooth. Spread over remaining strip. Cut into squares.

12. Melt Welch's® Concord Grape Jam and drizzle over all.

Mammoth Peanut Butter & Jelly Sandwich

Approximately 8 servings

1 round loaf French or Italian bread

Peanut butter

Welch's® Grape Jelly

Whipped cream cheese

Walnuts, chopped

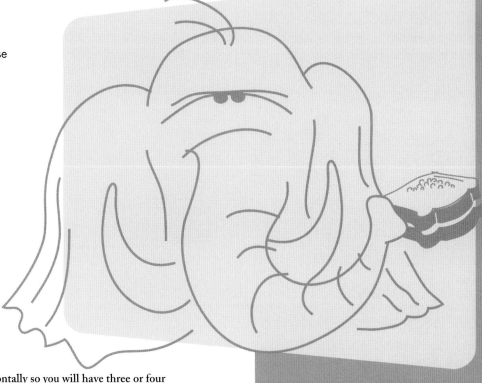

1. Slice the bread horizontally so you will have three or four layers, depending on the size of the loaf.

2. Spread all but the top layer with peanut butter and Welch's® Grape Jelly.

3. Assemble as you would a layer cake.

4. Cover generously with cream cheese, and sprinkle around the sides with chopped nuts.

5. Chill for 30 minutes or so. Slice into wedges.

Grape Tortoni Cups

12 servings

2 cups almond macaroon crumbs, firmly packed

1 cup Welch's® Concord Grape Jam

1 quart vanilla ice cream, slightly softened

1 cup heavy whipping cream, whipped

¼ cup Welch's® Concord Grape Jelly

Toppings of choice

1. In a bowl, combine macaroon crumbs and Welch's® Concord Grape Jam.

2. Mix until crumbs are well coated.

3. Spread mixture evenly over the bottom of 12 2-inch tortoni cups. (muffin/baking cups)

4. Cover with ice cream and top with swirls of whipped cream.

5. Place in freezer until cream is stiff. Remove from freezer about 5 minutes before serving time.

6. Dot with grape Welch's® Concord Grape Jelly.

Variation:

Top with colored or chocolate decorettes, coconut, slivered almonds, or chopped maraschino cherries.

Jelly Shells

36 servings

Favorite pastry recipe

1 Jar (10 oz.) Welch's® Concord Grape Jelly

Walnut, halves

1. Preheat oven to 425°F.

2. Press pastry into 36 1½-inch fluted molds. Flute edges, and prick all over with toothpick.

3. Bake on cookie sheet for 8 to 10 minutes, or until light golden brown.

4. When cool, fill tart shells with Welch's® Concord Grape Jelly.

5. Press walnut half into top of each.

Tip:

If you do not have molds, make tiny tart shells by shaping heavy aluminum foil over back of round, tablespoon-size measuring spoon and trim, allowing a ½-inch turn-back for rim.

Party Bon-Bons

1 package (7 oz.) vanilla wafers

1 can blanched almonds, finely chopped

1 cup flaked coconut

¾ cup Welch's® Concord Grape Jelly

35 maraschino cherries with stems

Bon-Bon Glaze

Bon-Bon Glaze

2½ cups confectioners sugar, sifted

½ cup unsalted butter

5 Tbsp. milk

1. Crush vanilla wafers into crumbs.

2. In a bowl, combine crumbs with almonds, coconut, and Welch's® Concord Grape Jelly. Stir until well blended.

3. Mold 1 tablespoon of the cookie mixture around each cherry, letting stem stand out on top.

4. Dip bon-bons into Bon-Bon Glaze and place on rack to drain.

5. Let stand at room temperature until dry.

Bon-Bon Glaze

1. Place sugar in a medium bowl; set aside.

2. In a small saucepan, melt butter over medium heat.

3. Immediately pour the melted butter into the bowl with the sugar.

4. Add the milk, and whisk until mixture is smooth.

5. Cover bowl, and store at room temperature until ready to use.

Macadamia Sauce

2 cups

1 cup Welch's® Grape Jam

1 tablespoon lemon juice

1 tablespoon pineapple juice

¼ cup crushed pineapple

½ cup macadamia nuts, chopped

1. In a saucepan, combine Welch's® Grape Jam, lemon juice, pineapple juice, and pineapple.

2. Cook over low heat, stirring constantly, just to simmer.

3. Remove from heat and cool slightly. Stir in nuts.

Tip:

Make a Macadamia Sherbet Parfait. Fill a parfait glass half full of ½-inch pound cake cubes. Spoon sauce over cake and top with lemon sherbet.

Petit Fours

6–8 servings

1 package white cake mix

Welch's® Grape Jelly

1½ cups granulated sugar

1½ Tbsp. corn syrup

¾ cup frozen, concentrated Welch's® Concord Grape Juice, thawed and undiluted

2 cups confectioners sugar, sifted

1. Preheat oven to 350°F. Line 15 x 10 x 1-inch pan with waxed paper.

2. In a bowl, prepare cake mix according to package directions. Pour into pan bake about 25 minutes.

3. Cool; remove from pan. Remove wax paper.

4. Cut cake into small squares, diamonds, circles, or other shapes.

5. Split each cake crosswise and fill with Welch's® Grape Jelly.

6. In a saucepan, combine sugar, corn syrup, and Welch's® Concord Grape Juice; cook at a boil until sugar is dissolved. Let stand 3 to 4 minutes.

7. Gradually stir in confectioners sugar and beat until smooth. Keep warm over hot water. Thin from time to time with 1 to 2 teaspoons water, if necessary.

8. Place cakes on cake rack with wax paper underneath to catch excess frosting.

9. Slowly pour frosting over cakes. Frosting drippings can be rewarmed and spooned again.

10. After frosting is firm, decorate with colored candies, shaved chocolate, nuts, tinted coconut, or candied fruits.

Metric Equivalency Charts

inches to millimeters and centimeters						
inches	mm	cm	inches	cm	inches	cm
⅛	3	0.3	9	22.9	30	76.2
¼	6	0.6	10	25.4	31	78.7
½	13	1.3	12	30.5	33	83.8
⅝	16	1.6	13	33.0	34	86.4
¾	19	1.9	14	35.6	35	88.9
⅞	22	2.2	15	38.1	36	91.4
1	25	2.5	16	40.6	37	94.0
1¼	32	3.2	17	43.2	38	96.5
1½	38	3.8	18	45.7	39	99.1
1¾	44	4.4	19	48.3	40	101.6
2	51	5.1	20	50.8	41	104.1
2½	64	6.4	21	53.3	42	106.7
3	76	7.6	22	55.9	43	109.2
3½	89	8.9	23	58.4	44	111.8
4	102	10.2	24	61.0	45	114.3
4½	114	11.4	25	63.5	46	116.8
5	127	12.7	26	66.0	47	119.4
6	152	15.2	27	68.6	48	121.9
7	178	17.8	28	71.1	49	124.5
8	203	20.3	29	73.7	50	127.0

yards to meters									
yards	meters	yards	meters	yards	meters	yards	meters	yards	meters
⅛	0.11	2⅛	1.94	4⅛	3.77	6⅛	5.60	8⅛	7.43
⅛	0.11	2⅛	1.94	4⅛	3.77	6⅛	5.60	8⅛	7.43
¼	0.23	2¼	2.06	4¼	3.89	6¼	5.72	8¼	7.54
⅜	0.34	2⅜	2.17	4⅜	4.00	6⅜	5.83	8⅜	7.66
⅝	0.46	2½	2.29	4½	4.11	6½	5.94	8½	7.77
⅝	0.57	2⅝	2.40	4⅝	4.23	6⅝	6.06	8⅝	7.89
¾	0.69	2¾	2.51	4¾	4.34	6¾	6.17	8¾	8.00
⅞	0.80	2⅞	2.63	4⅞	4.46	6⅞	6.29	8⅞	8.12
1	0.91	3	2.74	5	4.57	7	6.40	9	8.23
1¼	1.03	3¼	2.86	5⅛	4.69	7¼	6.52	9⅛	8.34
1¼	1.14	3¼	2.97	5¼	4.80	7¼	6.63	9¼	8.46
1⅜	1.26	3⅜	3.09	5⅜	4.91	7⅜	6.74	9⅜	8.57
1½	1.37	3½	3.20	5½	5.03	7½	6.86	9½	8.69
1⅝	1.49	3⅝	3.31	5⅝	5.14	7⅝	6.97	9⅝	8.80
1¾	1.60	3¾	3.43	5¾	5.26	7¾	7.09	9¾	8.92
1⅞	1.71	3⅞	3.54	5⅞	5.37	7⅞	7.20	9⅞	9.03
2	1.83	4	3.66	6	5.49	8	7.32	10	9.14

Index

Index continued